Clean Water Act

ESSENTIALS

Third Edition

Allison Rumsey, Joel M. Gross,
Ethan Shenkman, and Edward McTiernan

AMERICAN BAR ASSOCIATION
Environment Energy and
Resources Section

Cover design by Mary Anne Kulchawik/ABA Design

Printed in the United States of America.

26 25 24 23 22   5 4 3 2 1

A catalog record for this book is available from the Library of Congress.

Discounts are available for books ordered in bulk. Special consideration is given to state bars, CLE programs, and other bar-related organizations. Inquire at Book Publishing, ABA Publishing, American Bar Association, 321 N. Clark Street, Chicago, Illinois 60654-7598.

www.shopABA.org

Contents

About the Authors

Allison Rumsey

Allison Rumsey is a partner in the Washington, D.C., office of Arnold & Porter, and is a member of the firm's Environmental Practice Group. She represents clients in state and federal regulatory enforcement actions, class action and citizen suit lawsuits, and business disputes. She represented BP in the Deepwater Horizon matter as it related to government enforcement under the Clean Water Act and Oil Pollution Act. She also represents a shipping company in the Huntington Bay oil spill. Allison also assists clients in navigating and, where there is litigation defending, the permitting process under the environmental laws applicable to large infrastructure and other projects. Prior to joining the firm, she was Counsel to the Assistant Attorney General, Environment and Natural Resources Division of the U.S. Department of Justice.

Ethan Shenkman

Ethan Shenkman is a partner in the Washington, D.C., office of Arnold & Porter, and is a member of the firm's Environmental Practice Group. Nationally known for his work with climate change policy and energy transition, he advises on renewable fuels, carbon capture and sequestration, methane regulation, the phaseout of HFCs, and renewable energy permitting. He also regularly represents clients in trial and appellate court, and in regulatory matters before federal and state agencies. Prior to joining the firm, he served as Deputy General Counsel at the EPA and, prior to that, as Deputy Assistant Attorney General at the Environment and Natural Resources Division of the U.S. Department of Justice.

Joel M. Gross

Joel Gross is a senior counsel in the Washington, D.C., office of Arnold & Porter, and is a member of the firm's Environmental Practice Group. Joel represents and advises clients in litigation and nonlitigation matters under federal and state environmental laws, with a special emphasis on compliance and enforcement issues. Prior to joining Arnold & Porter, he was chief of the Environmental Enforcement Section of the U.S. Department of Justice, where he handled and supervised many Clean Water Act matters. He also worked with EPA on policy and legislative initiatives related to the Clean Water Act.

Ed McTiernan

Ed McTiernan is a partner in the New York office of Arnold & Porter, and is a member of the firm's Environmental Practice Group. He is an environmental litigator who focuses on state and federal regulatory issues, including site remediation, Brownfield redevelopment, natural resource damages, energy and infrastructure projects, as well as wastewater and stormwater permitting and defense of enforcement proceedings. Prior to joining the firm, he served as the Deputy Commissioner and General Counsel at the New York State Department of Environmental Conservation.

1 Executive Summary

The Federal Water Pollution Control Act, commonly known as the Clean Water Act (CWA),[1] is the primary federal statute regulating water pollution, with the goal of protecting the water resources of the United States. The CWA is intended to protect the quality of lakes, streams, and other waters for recreational use, maintenance of aquatic life, and use as drinking water sources.[2]

Although, as discussed in Chapter 2, the Clean Water Act's beginnings are founded in 19th-century law, major revisions enacted in 1972 formed the basis of today's Clean Water Act. The CWA is comprehensive in its coverage of discharges of pollutants into the waters of the United States, its stated goal being to "restore and maintain the chemical, physical, and biological integrity of the Nation's waters."[3] It is a complex statute that addresses various pathways by which pollutants are discharged into the nation's waters, covering municipal discharges of domestic wastewater, both treated and untreated, that contain biological and other pollution; the discharge by industry of process wastewater containing chemicals and other pollutants; discharges from livestock operations containing animal wastes; the direct and indirect discharge of polluted stormwater from all types of facilities; the filling of waters, especially wetlands, for development; and spills from vessels, pipelines, and industrial facilities.

As described in Chapter 3, the central provision of the Clean Water Act is the prohibition of the "discharge of any pollutant"

1. 33 U.S.C. §§ 1251 *et seq.*

2. Another federal statute, the Safe Drinking Water Act, 42 U.S.C. §§ 300f–300j-27, regulates entities that provide public drinking water.

3. CWA § 101(a), 33 U.S.C. § 1251(a).

into waters of the United States by any person without a permit. This prohibition, set forth in section 301, means that no one is allowed to "add" any "pollutants" (a broadly defined term including such things as solid waste, biological materials, and heat) from a "point source" (encompassing all manners of discrete conveyances) into "navigable waters" (defined as the "waters of the United States," a much debated and litigated term).

The CWA provides for four types of permits, two of which are most prevalent. The first, administered by the U.S. Environmental Protection Agency (EPA), is the National Pollutant Discharge Elimination System (NPDES) permit, which allows certain kinds of discharges of pollutants into the waters of the United States. The NPDES permit process is introduced in Chapter 4, and the standards used to determine limits in NPDES permits are discussed in Chapters 5, 6, and 7. Those standards are both technology-based and water quality-driven. Chapter 5 discusses technology-based standards that, in effect, make it so that a particular type of facility, be it a sewage treatment plant or a steel mill, would have the same discharge limitations wherever it is located. Chapter 6 discusses water quality-driven standards, including antidegradation policies and the concept of total maximum daily loads. Water quality-driven standards potentially effect stricter limitations for facilities that discharge to more polluted waters. Chapter 7 discusses the unique provisions applicable to publicly owned treatment works (POTWs), generally sewage systems owned by municipalities, including pretreatment requirements for industrial facilities that discharge to a POTW (rather than directly into navigable waters).

The second most common permit is for "dredge and fill" discharges. This permit, administered by the U.S. Army Corps of Engineers, is issued under section 404 of the CWA. The wetlands protection programs have been especially controversial because of the tension between protecting wetlands, which have enormous environmental benefits, and allowing the development and use of private property. The protection of wetlands and the issuance of section 404 permits are discussed in Chapter 8.

Oil and hazardous substances have the capacity to create such damaging effects, if discharged, that there are special provisions regulating their handling, reporting, and disposal. These are discussed in Chapter 9.

Chapters 10 and 11 address pollution transported to waters by rain and other wet-weather conditions. Controlling wet-weather discharges is an especially important issue in the protection of water bodies. Nationwide, there are thousands of cases of water quality impairment attributable to polluted stormwater, whether from farmland, streets, parking lots, construction sites, or other sources.[4] Chapter 10 discusses the regulation of wet-weather discharges from point sources, specifically from municipal and industrial sources. In the municipal context, some sanitary sewer systems that are separate from stormwater systems experience unwanted inflow of stormwater into the collection systems, causing the POTW to exceed treatment capacity. The resulting "sanitary sewer overflows" (SSOs) cause discharges of untreated sewage into receiving waters. Other sewer systems, typically in older cities, have combined sewer systems, in which sanitary sewage and stormwater are transported together. These combined systems often have wet-weather discharges of untreated sewage caused by the additional precipitation, referred to as "combined sewer overflows" (CSOs).

The CWA's program for addressing "nonpoint" source discharges, which include such things as agricultural and industrial runoff, is discussed in Chapter 11.

The methods available for ensuring compliance are key to achieving the CWA's water quality goals. The Clean Water Act is essentially a self-monitoring statute; permit holders are required to monitor their discharges and report them to the appropriate regulatory agency. Enforcement tools available to the federal and state governments include civil penalties, injunctive relief, and criminal sanctions. To a certain extent, these tools are also available to citizen plaintiffs seeking to enforce the CWA. The enforcement mechanisms provided for in the CWA are discussed in Chapter 12.

4. *See Impaired Waters and Stormwater*, EPA, https://www.epa.gov/tmdl/impaired-waters-and-stormwater (last updated Nov. 15, 2021).

2 The History of the Clean Water Act

2.1 Foundations of the Modern Act

The modern-day Clean Water Act (CWA) originated more than a century ago, with the oldest federal pollution law in the United States: the 1899 Rivers and Harbors Act, often referred to as the "Refuse Act."[1] Although primarily enacted to ensure the free and open navigability of U.S. waters, the Refuse Act also prohibited the discharge of "refuse matter of any kind or description whatever other than that flowing from streets and sewers and passing therefrom in a liquid state, into any navigable water of the United States" and granted authority to the Secretary of the Army to permit such discharges under prescribed conditions.[2] The Refuse Act thus became an early tool for controlling water pollution. Indeed, in 1959, the Supreme Court held in *United States v. Republic Steel Corp.* that the Refuse Act could be utilized to address wastewater discharges to the Calumet River in Illinois from a steel mill.[3] Importantly, however, the Court grounded its holding on the issue of navigability, rather than pollution. The Court found that the discharges had reduced the depth of the river's channel, which in turn obstructed its "navigable capacity."[4]

Historically, a major concern of the federal government has been the spread of communicable diseases from the inappropriate discharge of sewage containing human waste near drinking water intakes. Consequently, the federal government long has been

1. 33 U.S.C. §§ 407 *et seq.*
2. *Id.* § 407.
3. 362 U.S. 482 (1960).
4. *Id.* at 489–90.

involved with funding the construction of publicly owned sewage treatment works (POTWs). With an increase in industrialization, the goal of protecting the nation's waters from *chemical* contamination received greater attention, culminating in the enactment of the 1948 Federal Water Pollution Control Act.[5] While Congress designed the 1948 Act to control water pollution, implementation was through state-led water quality–based efforts, with the federal role mainly confined to supporting research and financing of treatment plants. Congress tasked state governors to enforce the act by using a cumbersome conference procedure, which consisted of (1) a conference of all affected state and interstate water pollution control agencies, with or without the polluter; (2) a recommendation by the Federal Water Pollution Control Administration (FWPCA) (a predecessor to the U.S. Environmental Protection Agency (EPA)) to the state agency to take a specific action within six months; and (3) a formal hearing before a board appointed by the FWPCA administrator, with the polluter called to the hearing in the event that the problem was not resolved by the state. Thereafter, the act left enforcement to the discretion of the FWPCA administrator. If the polluter declined to take abatement measures, the administrator could, but was not required to, request that the attorney general bring a suit for abatement on behalf of the United States. The attorney general similarly had discretion as to whether to proceed with the action. As of 1971, only one case had reached the courts.[6] Congress attempted to bolster the 1948 Act with the Water Quality Act of 1965, which required each state and territory to develop standards for water quality within its boundaries by July 1, 1967.[7] More than four years after that deadline, however, only half of the jurisdictions had fully approved standards.[8] Without water pollution control standards for these jurisdictions, no adequate federal enforcement was possible.

By 1970, however, an environmental consciousness had begun to emerge in the United States: concern about air and water pollution moved from tenth place in 1969 to fifth place in 1970, a shift that was symbolized by the first Earth Day in

5. Pub. L. No. 845, 62 Stat. 1155 (1948).
6. *See* S. Rep. No. 92-414, at 5 (1971).
7. Pub. L. No. 89-234, 79 Stat. 903 (1965).
8. *See* S. Rep. No. 92-414, at 4 (1971).

1970.[9] The movement derived in part from a number of significant national pollution events, including the January 1969 oil spill off the coast of Santa Barbara, California, and the June 1969 fire in the heavily polluted Cuyahoga River in Ohio.[10] Many of the nation's waterways had become severely polluted, with those near urban areas being unfit for most purposes.[11] Rivers, lakes, and streams were being used for waste disposal rather than to support human life and health.[12] In response to these developments, the Subcommittee on Air and Water Pollution (under the Senate Committee on Public Works) held hearings in 1970 and 1971. The Committee found that "the national effort to abate and control water pollution has been inadequate in every vital aspect."[13] Based on these findings, Congress, in 1972, implemented a major overhaul of the 1948 Act, the CWA. In urging President Nixon—whose veto of the legislation ultimately was overridden—to approve the amendments, then-EPA administrator William Ruckelshaus wrote: "More so than any other, water is our most important resource. It sustains our industry, our farms, our commerce, our enjoyment, and our lives. It is also most unforgiving if it is abused. The effects linger and, if continued, multiply."[14]

2.2 The 1972 Amendments: The New CWA

Congress's stated objective in enacting the new Clean Water Act was to "restore and maintain the chemical, physical, and biological integrity of the nation's waters."[15] The legislation represented a shift in regulatory philosophy, from a focus on water quality

9. *See* John C. Whitaker, *Earth Day Recollections: What It Was Like when the Movement Took Off*, EPA J., July/Aug. 1988, https://archive.epa.gov/epa/about epa/earth-day-recollections-what-it-was-when-movement-took.html.

10. *See, e.g.*, Jack Lewis, *The Spirit of the First Earth Day*, EPA J., Jan./Feb. 1990, at 8.

11. *See* S. Rep. No. 92-414, at 7 (1971).

12. *See id.*

13. *Id.*

14. Costs of Construction of Publicly Owned Wastewater Treatment Works 1973 "Needs" Survey, U.S. Environmental Protection Agency: Hearings Before the Subcomm. on Water Res. of the Comm. on Pub. Works, 93d Cong. 38–53 (1973) (letter from William Ruckelshaus, Adm'r, Env't. Prot. Agency, to the Office of Mgmt. & Budget, Oct. 11, 1972, Recommending Presidential Approval of S. 2770, the Federal Water Pollution Control Act Amendments of 1972).

15. CWA § 101(a), 33 U.S.C. § 1251(a).

standards established by states to a focus on a nationwide "clean waters" approach through institution of uniform technology-based standards as a function of industrial categories and classes.[16] The CWA established a number of goals and benchmarks, including the elimination of all discharges of pollutants into waters by the year 1985.[17] More specifically, the 1972 amendments endeavored to:

- Obtain a level of water quality that was protective of fish, wildlife, and recreational use of water by July 1, 1983;
- Provide increased federal financial assistance to construct POTW;
- Develop and implement waste treatment management planning processes in each state;
- Provide funds for research and development of technology to eliminate the discharge of pollutants; and
- Develop and implement programs for the control of nonpoint sources of pollution.[18]

The amendments included three key features to achieve these goals. First, the CWA included a prohibition against discharges of any pollutant into the "waters of the United States" absent specific authorization,[19] which primarily came through the National Pollutant Discharge Elimination System (NPDES).[20] The scope of "waters of the United States"—the term that serves as the gatekeeper for the application of federal CWA requirements—has, as discussed briefly in this chapter and in more detail in Chapter 3, turned out to be one of the most debated and litigated issues under the CWA. As discussed further in Chapter 3, NPDES provides for the issuance of permits that allow for the discharge of certain pollutants subject to certain effluent limits. NPDES permits are primarily issued to industrial dischargers and POTWs. Second, the 1972 amendments outlined pretreatment standards for "indirect dischargers," or those who discharge to a POTW rather than

---

16. *See* Frank P. Grad, Treatise on Environmental Law § 3.03[2][a-1], Lexis (Release No. 89) [hereinafter Grad Treatise].
17. CWA § 101(a)(1), 33 U.S.C. § 1251(a)(1).
18. CWA § 101(a)(2)–(7), 33 U.S.C. § 1251(a)(2)–(7).
19. CWA § 301, 33 U.S.C. § 1311.
20. CWA § 402, 33 U.S.C. § 1342.

directly into navigable waters. Third, the CWA became federally enforceable, shifting both the determination of the level of allowable discharges and permitting authority from states to EPA.[21]

2.2.1 Effluent Limitations

In conjunction with the NPDES process, the 1972 amendments provided for uniform technology-based effluent limitations to all discharges of pollutants, to be determined by the EPA administrator for various classes and categories dischargers. The amendments contemplated implementation of these effluent limits in two stages: by 1977, effluent limits for industrial dischargers would be based on the best practicable control technology currently available (BPT); and, by 1983, they would be based on a more stringent standard known as best available technology economically achievable (BAT). Congress similarly bifurcated implementation of the effluent limits for POTWs, calling for "secondary treatment" by 1977 and for limits based on "best practicable waste treatment technology" by 1983.[22] The 1972 amendments also authorized EPA to require more stringent limits where specific water bodies—classified or designated as impaired—could not otherwise achieve desired water quality standards.

2.2.2 Water Quality–Based Program

In addition to the technology-based requirements described in Section 2.2.1 of this chapter, the 1972 amendments created a comprehensive and complementary water quality–based program. This program included the establishment of national water quality standards, procedures for establishing total daily maximum loads for impaired waters, and a continuous state planning process for protection of water quality.

---

21. States can be authorized to take over the permitting process only where the state has satisfied prescribed conditions. As of July 2021, only three states—Massachusetts, New Hampshire, and New Mexico—lack NPDES permitting authority. Moreover, American Samoa, the District of Columbia, Guam, Johnston Atoll, Midway Island, the Northern Mariana Islands, Puerto Rico, and Wake Island do not have NPDES permitting authority. *See NPDES State Program Authority*, EPA, https://www.epa.gov/npdes/npdes-state-program-authority (last updated July 7, 2021).

22. Primary treatment refers to the physical treatment through settling, filtration, and other means. Secondary treatment involves more advanced treatments, usually including biological treatment of sewage.

2.2.3 Monitoring and Enforcement of the CWA

Another significant change from the 1948 Act was the authorization of the federal government, states, and citizens to enforce the prohibitions of the CWA. The CWA's auditing mechanisms, mainly self-reporting requirements that may also include site inspections by regulatory agencies, provide the basis for enforcement actions brought to obtain civil and criminal penalties as well as injunctive relief.

2.2.4 Construction Grant Programs

The 1972 amendments also established a grant program to fund up to 75% of the costs of construction of sewage treatment plants across the country.

2.3 The 1977 Amendments

Congress amended the CWA in 1977. The amended CWA required that BAT limitations for toxic pollutants and best available conventional pollutant control technology (BCT) limitations for conventional pollutants be achieved by July 1, 1984. The 1977 amendments also added provisions for best management practices, removal credits for pretreatment standards, and modifications of BAT requirements for nontoxic pollutants. Finally, the 1977 amendments emphasized that the states bear the initial responsibility for management and enforcement, with EPA having ultimate enforcement authority.[23]

2.4 The 1987 Amendments

The 1987 amendments phased out the construction grants program and introduced the State Revolving Fund (SRF). The SRF finances not only municipal wastewater collection and treatment

23. *See* Grad Treatise, *supra* note 16, § 3.03.

facilities but also improvements in urban stormwater and nonpoint source management practices, estuarine and groundwater protection programs, and sanitary sewer overflow control projects. Since its inception, the SRF has extended assistance in the form of more than 42,000 low-interest loans totaling over $145 billion.[24]

Another significant component of the 1987 amendments was the Water Quality Act of 1987,[25] which strengthened the regulation of point source stormwater discharges, an area that had not been adequately addressed in the CWA.[26] The Water Quality Act created a two-phase approach to regulating stormwater. The first phase, for which EPA issued regulations in 1990, regulated stormwater discharged from point sources relating to industrial activity, large municipal sources, and other sources of significant contributions to pollution. The second phase required regulation of all other stormwater discharges no earlier than October 1, 1994.[27] EPA promulgated these regulations in December 1999.[28]

2.5 The Oil Pollution Act of 1990

In response to the March 24, 1989, *Exxon Valdez* spill, during which more than 11 million gallons of crude oil were released into Alaska's Prince William Sound, Congress began to evaluate the adequacy of the CWA to address releases of oil from vessels and offshore facilities. The Senate Committee on Environment

24. *See Clean Water State Revolving Fund (CWSRF)*, EPA, https://www.epa.gov/cwsrf (last updated July 3, 2021).

25. Pub. L. No. 100-4, 101 Stat. 76 (1987).

26. Following the 1972 amendments, EPA promulgated NPDES permit regulations exempting uncontaminated stormwater discharges from regulation, as their regulation was thought to be administratively infeasible. The Court of Appeals for the District of Columbia Circuit set aside those regulations in its ruling in *Natural Resources Defense Council v. Costle*, 568 F.2d 1369, 1377 (D.C. Cir. 1977). EPA issued rules governing stormwater discharges in 1980, 1982, 1984, and 1985, but the 1987 amendments represented the first legislative effort to regulate stormwater discharges.

27. The original moratorium on permitting stormwater discharges for phase two point sources was to end October 31, 1992; this was extended to October 1, 1994.

28. *See* EPA Storm Water Phase II Final Rule, 64 Fed. Reg. 68,722 (Dec. 8, 1999).

and Public Works determined that, under pre-*Valdez* law, costs associated with releases of oil were relatively low, and the oil industry treated such expenditures as an accepted cost of doing business. Thus, Congress lacked an effective statutory tool to encourage greater industry efforts to prevent spills.[29] In recognition of this circumstance, Congress enacted the Oil Pollution Act of 1990 (OPA) to provide authority for the determination of liability, cleanup, and penalties for oil pollution.[30] Congress also created the Oil Spill Liability Trust Fund to pay for spill cleanup and to compensate injured parties.[31] The OPA represents a significant development in the history of water pollution regulation. While legislatively distinct from the CWA, the OPA is closely related to section 311 of the CWA, which addresses oil spills and is discussed in Chapter 9.

2.6 Nonlegislative Developments

In the 30 years since the passage of the OPA, there have not been such significant legislative changes to the CWA. Still, there has been substantial activity impacting the CWA as successive presidential administrations have sought to implement their clean water priorities, and as cases addressing the scope of the CWA have been adjudicated by courts, including the Supreme Court.

For example, in 1998, President Clinton announced the Clean Water Action Plan, intended to create a coordinated effort among federal, state, tribal, and local communities, individuals, and businesses to focus on water quality standards and protections.[32] The plan's objective was to view water quality from a watershed approach and to emphasize

29. *See* S. Rep. No. 101-94, at 3 (July 28, 1989).
30. Pub. L. No. 101-380, 104 Stat. 484 (1990).
31. The Oil Spill Liability Trust Fund was established by 26 U.S.C. § 9509 and is funded in large part by revenue received under 26 U.S.C. § 4611, which taxes certain refiners of crude oil and distributors of petroleum products. *See* 26 U.S.C. § 9509(b)(1).
32. Clean Water Action Plan: Restoring and Protecting America's Waters (1998), https://bit.ly/3etnnPt.

> the function and condition of watersheds; the incorporation of watershed goals in federal agency planning and programs; the enhancement of pollution prevention; the improvement of monitoring; the restoration of watersheds; the identification of waters of exceptional value; and the expanding collaboration among federal agencies, states, tribes, and interested stakeholders.[33]

The plan was, for the most part, not implemented.

In October 2009, during the Obama administration, EPA administrator Lisa Jackson issued a similarly titled Clean Water Act Action Plan, related to collaboration among state and federal stakeholders regarding implementation of the NPDES permitting and enforcement program.[34] As discussed in Chapter 3, the Obama administration also devoted significant resources to seeking to extensively spell out by rule the scope of "waters of the United States," after that term had been addressed by the Supreme Court in 2006 in a decision that raised as many questions as it answered.[35] The Obama administration's "Clean Water Rule: Definition of Water of the United States"[36] was issued in 2015, immediately challenged in multiple courts, stayed in more than half of the states, and eventually repealed and replaced by the Trump administration.[37] The Trump administration's "Navigable Waters Protection Rule" also faced challenges in multiple courts and was stayed nationwide.[38] The issue is being revisited by the Biden administration, which in December 2021 proposed to return to the regulatory regime in place before the Clean Water Rule while continuing to consult with stakeholders on implementation and future regulatory actions.[39] The scope of "waters of the United States" will no doubt continue to be the subject of attention for years to come.

---

33. *See* Grad Treatise, *supra* note 16, § 3.03[2][a-2][ii].

34. *See* EPA, Clean Water Act Action Plan (Oct. 15, 2009), https://www.epa.gov/sites/default/files/documents/actionplan101409.pdf.

35. *See* Rapanos v. United States, 547 U.S. 715 (2006).

36. 80 Fed. Reg. 37,053 (June 29, 2015).

37. See 84 Fed. Reg. 22,250 (Apr. 21, 2020).

38. Pascua Yaqui Tribe v. EPA, 2021 WL 3855977, __ F. Supp. 3d __ (D. Ariz. Aug. 30, 2021).

39. 86 Fed. Reg. 69,372 (Dec. 7, 2021); see Press Release, EPA, EPA and Army Take Action to Provide Certainty for the Definition of WOTUS (Nov. 18, 2021), https://www.epa.gov/newsreleases/epa-and-army-take-action-provide-certainty-definition-wotus.

2.7 The CWA at 50

As the CWA reaches its fiftieth anniversary, the improvements to the quality of American waterways are both significant and measurable. For example, between the time of the CWA's enactment and 2012, the number of people provided with advanced wastewater treatment increased from 7.8 million to 127.7 million.[40] In 1969, Ohio's Cuyahoga River was so filled with oily waste and industrial pollution that it caught fire. *Time* magazine described it as the river that "oozes rather than flows." Today, the Cuyahoga is known as the "river of recovery" due to restoration efforts over the last four decades.[41] Moreover, in a study of U.S. lakes that compared conditions in 2007 to conditions in the 1970s, half the surveyed lakes featured reductions in nutrient concentrations, while 25 percent showed improved trophic status.[42]

When the CWA was enacted, the Potomac River was too dirty to swim in, Lake Erie was dying, and the Cuyahoga River was so polluted it burst into flames. Many rivers and beaches were little more than open sewers. Enactment of the CWA dramatically improved the health of rivers, lakes, and coastal waters. It stopped billions of pounds of pollution from fouling the water and doubled the number of waterways deemed safe for fishing and swimming. Today, many rivers, lakes, and coasts are thriving centers of healthy communities.

Despite these achievements, deteriorated conditions remain in many waterways. Section 305 of the CWA requires states to report the quality and characteristics of navigable waters within their boundaries to EPA every two years.[43] EPA compiles the information into the National Water Quality Inventory, which

40. *See* EPA, EPA-830-R-15005, Clean Watersheds Needs Survey 2012: Report to Congress 25 (Jan. 2016), https://www.epa.gov/sites/default/files/2015-12/documents/cwns_2012_report_to_congress-508-opt.pdf.

41. *See* Christopher Maag, *From the Ashes of '69, a River Reborn*, N.Y. Times, June 20, 2009, at A18. For a different historical perspective on the reality and importance of the Cuyahoga River fire, see John Cronin, *The Cuyahoga Fire at Fifty: A False History Obscures the Real Water Crisis that Never Ceased*, 9 J. Envtl. Stud. & Scis. 340 (2019).

42. *See* EPA, EPA 841-R-09-001, National Lakes Assessment: A Collaborative Survey of the Nation's Lakes 75 (2009), https://www.epa.gov/sites/default/files/2013-11/documents/nla_newlowres_fullrpt.pdf.

43. 33 U.S.C. § 1315.

it reports to Congress. In its report to Congress issued in August 2017, EPA reported that in the United States:

- 46% of river and stream miles are in poor biological condition, with phosphorus and nitrogen being the most widespread of the chemical stressors assessed;
- 21% of lakes are hypereutrophic, meaning that they have the highest levels of nutrients, algae, and plants;
- 18% of coastal and Great Lakes waters are in poor biological condition and 14% are rated poor based on a water quality index; and
- 32% of wetland areas are in poor biological condition, with leading stressors including surface hardening (soil compaction) and vegetation removal.[44]

Thus, while the CWA has played a pivotal role in reducing water pollution in the United States, continued implementation and enforcement of the requirements of the CWA will be essential for further progress to be made.

44. EPA, EPA 841-R-16-011, National Water Quality Inventory: Report to Congress (Aug. 2017), https://www.epa.gov/sites/default/files/2017-12/documents/305brtc_finalowow_08302017.pdf.

3 General Prohibition of Discharges

3.1 Introduction

Section 301 sets forth the central provision of the Clean Water Act (CWA): the prohibition of the discharge of pollutants from a point source into navigable waters of the United States, unless in compliance with the specific and limited authorizations in the CWA.[1] The meaning of each of the terms contained within section 301 is pivotal in determining whether a prohibited discharge has occurred. If a discharge falls within the defined terms of the prohibition, it is barred unless one of the authorizations listed in section 301(a) applies.

3.2 The Prohibition Defined

The actual language of the prohibition is simple: "Except as in compliance with this section and sections 1312, 1316, 1317, 1328, 1342, and 1344 of this title, the discharge of any pollutant by any person shall be unlawful."[2] The threshold inquiry—whether the prohibition of section 301 applies—requires a review of the broadly defined terms upon which the prohibition

1. *See* CWA § 301(a), 33 U.S.C. § 1311(a).
2. *See* CWA § 301(a), 33 U.S.C. § 1311(a). As discussed more fully in Chapter 4, the most extensive exception is that found in section 402, which allows certain discharges of pollutants in certain amounts if a permit has been issued for such discharges. *See* CWA § 402, 33 U.S.C. § 1342. Another major exception is found in section 404, providing for authorizations of the discharge of dredge and fill material. *See* CWA § 404, 33 U.S.C. § 1344.

is premised. The CWA defines "discharge of a pollutant" as "any *addition* of any *pollutant* to *navigable waters* from any *point source*," or "any addition of any pollutant to the waters of the contiguous zone or the ocean from any point source other than a vessel or other floating craft."[3] Focusing on the first half of that definition, there are thus four essential elements to the application of the prohibition related to the use of the terms "addition," "pollutant," "navigable waters," and "point source." These are discussed in turn.

3.2.1 Addition

The Clean Water Act does not define the term "addition," which has been the subject of considerable judicial interpretation. Courts have held, for example, that "sidecasting," or the placement of dredged materials to the sides of ditches excavated in a wetland, constitutes an "addition,"[4] while "incidental fallback" associated with dredging activities, such as "when a bucket used to excavate material from the bottom of a river, stream, or wetland is raised and soils or sediments fall from the bucket back into the water," does not.[5]

Another issue evaluated by a number of courts is whether the "addition" element is met where polluted water from one water body is diverted and discharged into another water body. In *South Florida Water Management District v. Miccosukee Tribe*, the Supreme Court considered whether a pumping facility in the Everglades that transferred phosphorus-laden water from a canal to a nearby reservoir required a National Pollutant Discharge Elimination System (NPDES) permit.[6] The Court indicated that such a transfer might be an "addition" requiring an NPDES permit, but only if the two water bodies were truly distinct, and ultimately remanded for further factual consideration of the distinctiveness issue.[7] In *Catskill Mountains Chapter of Trout Unlimited, Inc. v.*

3. CWA § 502(12), 33 U.S.C. § 1362(12) (emphasis added).

4. *See* United States v. Cundiff, 555 F.3d 200, 213–14 (6th Cir. 2009); United States v. Deaton, 209 F.3d 331 (4th Cir. 2000).

5. *See* Nat'l Mining Ass'n v. U.S. Army Corps of Eng'rs, 145 F.3d 1399, 1403 (D.C. Cir. 1998).

6. 541 U.S. 95 (2004).

7. *See id.* at 111–12. The Court also addressed an argument advanced by the United States as *amicus curiae* that all navigable waters in the United States should

City of New York, the Second Circuit likewise held that the transfer of turbid water from a water management tunnel into a creek constituted an "addition" requiring an NPDES permit.[8] In response to these and other decisions, in 2008, the U.S. Environmental Protection Agency (EPA) issued the Water Transfers Rule, which provides that transfers do not result in the "addition" of a pollutant and, accordingly, do not require NPDES permits.[9] Courts have upheld the Water Transfers Rule in response to challenges. For example, the Eleventh Circuit in *Friends of the Everglades v. South Florida Water Management District* held that the Water Transfers Rule was a reasonable construction of the CWA.[10] In a subsequent case, *Catskill Mountains Chapter of Trout Unlimited, Inc. v. U.S. EPA,* the Second Circuit *also upheld* the Water Transfers Rule as based on a reasonable interpretation of the CWA and not arbitrary and capricious.[11] In *Los Angeles County Flood Control District v. Natural Resources Defense Council, Inc.*, the Supreme Court held that flow of water from an improved portion of a navigable waterway into an unimproved portion of the same waterway does not qualify as a discharge of pollutants under the CWA.[12]

3.2.2 Pollutant

The term "pollutant" is broadly defined to include any waste discharged into water, irrespective of source, including dredged spoil, solid waste, incinerator residue, sewage, garbage, sewage sludge, munitions, chemical wastes, biological materials, radioactive materials, wrecked or discarded equipment, rock, sand, cellar dirt, and industrial, municipal, and agricultural waste.[13] Heat also is listed as a pollutant, meaning that an industrial facility discharging noncontact cooling water, which may contain no chemical

be considered "unitarily for purposes of NPDES permitting," meaning that there is no "addition" when water is transferred between navigable waters "even if one water body were polluted and the other pristine." *Id.* at 106. Because this "unitary waters" issue had not been raised below, the Court declined to decide it, and remanded that issue as well. *See id.*

8. 451 F.3d 77, 83–84 (2d Cir. 2006).
9. *See* 73 Fed. Reg. 33,697 (June 13, 2008).
10. 570 F.3d 1210 (11th Cir. 2009), cert. denied, 562 U.S. 1082 (2010).
11. 846 F.3d 492 (2d Cir. 2017), *cert. denied,* 138 S. Ct. 1164–65 (2018).
12. 568 U.S. 78 (2013).
13. CWA § 502(6), 33 U.S.C. § 1362(6).

contaminant but is warmer than the receiving water, is prohibited unless an exception applies.[14]

Courts have generally interpreted the term "pollutant" broadly,[15] finding, for instance, that pollutants can include bombs dropped from aircraft,[16] nonnative fish introduced into a receiving water,[17] and elements added to a water body that are naturally occurring, such as atmospheric gases caused by the operation of a dam.[18] EPA issued a final rule in 2006, exempting from CWA regulation the application of aquatic pesticides in compliance with the Federal Insecticide, Fungicide, and Rodenticide Act, based on EPA's interpretation of "pollutant" as not including pesticides in such circumstances.[19] The Sixth Circuit later vacated the rule in *National Cotton Council of America v. U.S. EPA*, finding that an NPDES permit is required where pesticides are applied, around, and over water unless the pesticides leave no residue.[20]

3.2.3 Navigable Waters

Whether a body of water is a "navigable water" is the pivotal question in determining federal versus state jurisdiction.[21] While "navigable waters" is the statutory term for the bodies of water (other than the waters of the contiguous zone or the ocean) that the CWA is intended to protect, the term as applied has little to do

---

14. *See* Catskill Mountains Chapter of Trout Unlimited, Inc. v. City of New York, 273 F.3d 481, 485 (2d Cir. 2001).

15. *See* Sierra Club, Lone Star Chapter v. Cedar Point Oil Co., 73 F.3d 546, 566–68 (5th Cir. 1996) (definition of "pollutant" is meant to "leave out very little"), *cert. denied*, 519 U.S. 811 (1996); *see also* Karen Wardzinski et al., *Water Pollution Control Under the National Pollutant Discharge Elimination System, in* The Clean Water Act Handbook (1994).

16. *See* Weinberger v. Romero-Barcelo, 456 U.S. 305 (1982).

17. *See* U.S. Pub. Int. Rsch. Grp. v. Atl. Salmon of Me., 215 F. Supp. 2d 239 (D. Me. 2002). *But see* Ass'n to Protect Hammersley, Eld & Totten Inlets v. Taylor Res., Inc., 299 F.3d 1007 (9th Cir. 2002) (shells, feces, and other materials produced by mussels growing on ropes suspended from floating rafts were not "pollutants," but were the natural byproducts of the shellfish life cycle).

18. *See* Nat'l Wildlife Fed'n v. Gorsuch, 530 F. Supp. 1291 (D.D.C. 1982) (the entrainment and solution of naturally occurring atmospheric gases in water caused by the operation of a dam and resulting in supersaturation lethal to aquatic life is considered a "pollutant"), *rev'd on other grounds*, 693 F.2d 156 (D.C. Cir. 1982). *But see* Bettls v. Town of Ontario, 800 F. Supp. 1113 (W.D.N.Y. 1992) (water itself is not a pollutant under the act).

19. *See* 71 Fed. Reg. 68,483 (Nov. 27, 2006).

20. 553 F.3d 927 (6th Cir. 2009). The court granted EPA's request for a two-year stay of its decision until April 9, 2011. *See* 76 Fed. Reg. 68,750, 68,753 (Nov. 7, 2011). In November 2011, EPA issued a final general NPDES permit for four specific pesticide use patterns. *See id.*

21. State v. Hoffman, 437 F. Supp. 114 (D. Wyo. 1977).

with actual navigability. Navigable waters is defined expansively as "waters of the United States, including the territorial seas,"[22] and the legislative history indicates that Congress intended the term to be as broad as constitutionally permissible under the Commerce Clause.[23] In the 1985 *Riverside Bayview Homes*[24] decision, the Supreme Court held that actual navigability of the water is of "limited import" and that the CWA covered "at least some waters that would not be deemed 'navigable' under the classical understanding of that term."[25]

The Supreme Court limited one aspect of the broad interpretation of navigable waters in *Solid Waste Agency of Northern Cook County (SWANCC) v. U.S. Army Corps of Engineers*.[26] The Court rejected the Migratory Bird Rule issued by the U.S. Army Corps of Engineers in 1986, which applied the definition of navigable waters to intrastate waters that "are or would be used as habitat by birds" that either are protected by Migratory Bird Treaties or that cross state lines. The Court found that the Migratory Bird Rule is not fairly supported by the CWA and could not be used as a basis for the Corps's jurisdiction.[27] The *SWANCC* decision stated that while the word "navigable" may have limited effect, it had to be given at least some effect, and so the Court was unwilling to extend the definition to non-navigable, isolated, intrastate ponds based solely on their use by migratory birds. The Court

---

22. CWA § 502(7), 33 U.S.C. § 1362(7). The term "territorial seas" means the belt of the seas measured from the line of ordinary low water along that portion of the coast that is in direct contact with the open sea and the line marking the seaward limit of inland waters, and extending seaward a distance of three miles. *See* CWA § 502(8), 33 U.S.C. § 1362(8).

23. The Conference Committee report accompanying the 1972 amendments stated: "The conferees fully intend that the term 'navigable water' be given the broadest possible constitutional interpretation unencumbered by agency determinations which have been made, or may be made for administrative purposes." H.R. Rep. No. 92-1465, at 144 (1972) (Conf. Rep.). The 1986/1988 regulatory definition of "waters of the United States" included seven categories: (1) Waters that have been or may be used in interstate or foreign commerce; (2) Interstate waters; (3) Intrastate waters if their "use, degradation, or destruction" would affect interstate or foreign commerce; (4) Impoundments of waters of the United States; (5) Tributaries of the waters in (1) through (4); (6) The territorial seas; and (7) Wetlands adjacent to waters in (1) through (6). 53 Fed. Reg. 20,764 (June 6, 1988) (Corps); 51 Fed. Reg. 41,216 (Nov. 13, 1986) (EPA).

24. United States v. Riverside Bayview Homes, Inc., 474 U.S. 121 (1985).

25. *Id.* at 133; *accord* United States v. Eidson, 108 F.3d 1336 (11th Cir. 1997), *cert. denied*, 522 U.S. 899 (1997); United States v. Oxford Royal Mushroom Prods., Inc., 487 F. Supp. 852 (E.D. Pa. 1980).

26. 531 U.S. 159 (2001).

27. *Id.* at 167.

distinguished its earlier decision in *Riverside Bayview Homes* as one in which the wetland in question actually abutted a navigable waterway.[28]

In 2006, the Court again considered the Corps's jurisdiction in *Rapanos v. United States, a case involving wetlands.*[29] While all of the justices agreed that the term "waters of the United States"—which the statute itself does not define—includes some waters that are not navigable in the traditional sense, they disagreed on the scope of the term, resulting in plurality, concurring, and dissenting opinions. A four-justice plurality, in an opinion authored by Justice Scalia, interpreted the term to include "relatively permanent, standing or continuously flowing bodies of water," excluding "channels through which water flows intermittently or ephemerally, or channels that periodically provide drainage for rainfall," but not necessarily "streams, rivers, or lakes that might dry up in extraordinary circumstances, such as drought," or "seasonal rivers, which contain continuous flow during some months of the year but no flow during dry months."[30] Justice Kennedy's concurrence concluded that the Corps's jurisdiction depended on whether there is a "significant nexus" between the wetlands at issue and the navigable water.[31] Justice Stevens's dissent, in which three justices joined, concluded that lower courts should find that the Corps has jurisdiction whenever either test is satisfied, because a majority of the court would have found jurisdiction under either test.[32]

The multiple opinions in *Rapanos* left the law in this area quite confused; some courts applied Justice Kennedy's "significant nexus" test,[33] while others followed the dissent, finding that jurisdiction exists over wetlands whenever either the plurality

---

28. *See id.* at 171–72. By basing its decision on a statutory interpretation ground, the Court did not need to reach the issue of whether Congress could constitutionally, under the Commerce Clause, apply the CWA to such isolated wetlands. An earlier court of appeals decision found, on the facts before it, that the exercise of federal jurisdiction was "unauthorized by the Clean Water Act as limited by the Commerce Clause and therefore is invalid." United States v. Wilson, 133 F.3d 251 (4th Cir. 1997).

29. 547 U.S. 715 (2006).

30. *Id.* at 732 n.5 (plurality opinion).

31. *Id.* at 786–87 (Kennedy, J., concurring).

32. *Id.* at 809–10 (Stevens, J., dissenting).

33. *See, e.g.*, S.F. Baykeeper v. Cargill Salt Div., 481 F.3d 700, 708 (9th Cir. 2007); United States v. Robison, 505 F.3d 1208, 1221 (11th Cir. 2007); United States v. Gerke Excavating, Inc., 464 F.3d 723, 724 (7th Cir. 2006).

or the "significant nexus" test is satisfied.[34] In an effort to clarify the issue, in December 2008, EPA and the Corps issued the joint *Rapanos* Guidance on the scope of the CWA. The *Rapanos* Guidance included a list of those waters over which the Corps would and would not assert jurisdiction, and a list of waters that would be analyzed under the "significant nexus" test.[35]

In April 2011, EPA and the Corps released further draft guidance to clarify the scope of jurisdiction under the CWA.[36] Approximately 230,000 public comments on the proposed guidance were submitted, with many recommending that the agencies propose a rule to clarify the scope of waters within the jurisdiction of the CWA. They did just that, proposing the "Waters of the United States" or WOTUS rule in April 2014.[37] The agencies received more than one million public comments on the proposed rule and conducted more than 400 meetings with stakeholders during the rulemaking process, culminating with the publication of the final rule in June 2015.[38] The Obama administration's 2015 WOTUS final rule—known as the Clean Water Rule—replaced the 1986/1988 regulatory definition of "waters of the United States"[39] and pre-2014 agency guidance documents.

The Clean Water Rule sought to provide "simpler, clearer, and more consistent approaches for identifying the geographic scope of the CWA," recognizing three general categories: (1) jurisdictional waters, (2) waters excluded from jurisdiction, and (3) "a narrow category of waters subject to case-specific analysis to determine whether they are jurisdictional."[40] Jurisdictional waters under the Clean Water Rule included traditional navigable waters, interstate waters, and the territorial seas, as well as their impoundments, tributaries, and adjacent waters. Waters excluded from jurisdiction

34. *See, e.g.*, United States v. Donovan, 661 F.3d 174, 182 (3d Cir. 2011); United States v. Johnson, 467 F.3d 56, 65–66 (1st Cir. 2006); United States v. Bailey, 571 F.3d 791, 799 (8th Cir. 2009).

35. *See* EPA, Clean Water Act Jurisdiction Following the U.S. Supreme Court's Decision in *Rapanos v. United States* & *Carabell v. United States* (2008), https://www.epa.gov/sites/production/files/2016-02/documents/cwa_jurisdiction_following_rapanos120208.pdf.

36. The draft guidance listed several types of waters categorically protected by the act as well as other types of waters that are protected if a fact-specific analysis determines they have a "significant nexus" to a traditional navigable water or interstate water.

37. *See* 79 Fed. Reg. 22,188 (Apr. 21, 2014).

38. *See* 80 Fed. Reg. 37,054 (June 29, 2015).

39. *See supra* note 23.

40. *See* 80 Fed. Reg. 37,054, 37,057 (June 29, 2015).

under WOTUS included prior converted cropland, waste treatment systems, certain ditches, groundwater and erosional features, stormwater control features, and cooling ponds created in dry land. Waters subject to case-specific analysis included "Prairie potholes, Carolina and Delmarva bays, pocosins, western vernal pools in California, and Texas coastal prairie wetlands," as well as waters within the 100-year floodplain or within 4,000 feet of the high tide line or the ordinary high water mark of traditional navigable waters, interstate waters, or the territorial seas.[41] These types of waters were jurisdictional if they had "a significant nexus to traditional navigable waters, interstate waters, or the territorial seas, either alone or in combination with similarly situated waters in the region."[42] "Significant nexus" was defined as "significantly affect[ing] the chemical, physical, or biological integrity" of the primary water body.[43] The agencies estimated that the Clean Water Rule would result in a small overall increase in the number of waters subject to federal jurisdiction compared to recent practice, but compared to historic practice and regulations, the scope of jurisdictional waters would decrease.[44]

The Clean Water Rule generated a significant backlash and political controversy. Almost immediately after it was issued, it was challenged in numerous courts, including federal district and appellate courts, and there was substantial confusion regarding whether the district courts or appellate courts had original jurisdiction to hear challenges to the rule. In August 2015, for example, the U.S. District Court for the District of North Dakota found it had jurisdiction and granted a preliminary stay of the rule for 13 states suing EPA and the Corps.[45] Then, in October 2015, the U.S. Court of Appeals for the Sixth Circuit issued a nationwide stay of the rule, pending its determination of its jurisdiction to consider the validity of the rule.[46] In February 2016, the Sixth Circuit ruled it had original jurisdiction and the rule was subject to direct appellate court review.[47] In January 2018, the U.S. Supreme Court

41. *Id.* at 37,059.
42. *Id.* at 37,058.
43. *Id.* at 37,109.
44. *See id.*
45. *See* North Dakota v. U.S. EPA, 127 F. Supp. 3d 1047 (D.N.D. 2015).
46. *See In re* EPA, 803 F.3d 804 (6th Cir. 2015).
47. *See In re* U.S. Dep't of Def. & U.S. EPA Final Rule: Clean Water Rule: Definition of "Waters of the United States," 817 F.3d 261 (6th Cir. 2016).

reversed the Sixth Circuit, holding that challenges to the rule were required to be brought in federal district courts.[48] Following the Supreme Court's decision, the Sixth Circuit vacated its nationwide stay and dismissed consolidated petitions for review of the rule due to lack of jurisdiction, while a patchwork of litigation challenging the rule proceeded in the federal district courts, with the rule being stayed in more than half of the states.[49]

While challenges to the Clean Water Rule were being litigated in the courts, the Trump administration sought to repeal and replace the rule. In February 2017, President Trump signed Executive Order 13778, "Restoring the Rule of Law, Federalism, and Economic Growth by Reviewing the 'Waters of the United States' Rule," directing EPA and the Corps to review and revise or rescind the WOTUS rule to narrow the scope of federal jurisdiction.[50] In accordance with the Executive Order, EPA and the Corps announced a two-step repeal and replacement process in July 2017.[51] The agencies completed step one of that process in October 2019, publishing a final rule rescinding the Clean Water Rule and recodifying the 1986/1988 regulatory definition that existed prior to 2015.[52] In April 2020, the agencies completed step two, publishing the final "Navigable Waters Protection Rule," narrowing the definition of "waters of the United States."[53]

The 2020 Navigable Waters Protection Rule purported to

> maintain[] federal authority over those waters that Congress determined should be regulated by the Federal government under its Commerce Clause powers, while adhering to Congress' policy directive to preserve States' primary authority over land and water resources.[54]

The rule defined "waters of the United States" as the territorial seas and waters used in interstate or foreign commerce, and their tributaries, lakes, ponds, impoundments, and adjacent wetlands.[55]

48. *See* Nat'l Ass'n of Mfrs. v. Dep't of Def., 138 S. Ct. 617 (2018).
49. *See In re* U.S. Dep't of Def., 713 F. App'x 489 (6th Cir. 2018); *see generally* Nat'l Conference of State Legislatures, Legal & Regulatory Timeline of "Waters of the United States" (2020), https://www.ncsl.org/Documents/standcomm/scnri/wotus_timeline.pdf.
50. *See* 82 Fed. Reg. 12,497 (Mar. 3, 2017).
51. *See* 82 Fed. Reg. 34,899 (July 27, 2017).
52. *See* 84 Fed. Reg. 56,626 (Oct. 22, 2019).
53. *See* 85 Fed. Reg. 22,250 (Apr. 21, 2020).
54. *Id.* at 22,250.
55. *Id.* at 22,251.

The rule excluded from the definition all other waters, including groundwater; ephemeral features; diffuse stormwater runoff; ditches; prior converted cropland; artificially irrigated areas; artificial lakes and ponds; water-filled depressions; stormwater control features; groundwater recharge, water reuse, and wastewater recycling structures; and waste treatment systems.[56]

Numerous lawsuits challenging the 2020 Navigable Waters Protection Rule were filed. In August 2021, a federal district court in Arizona vacated the rule nationwide.[57] In response, EPA and the Corps halted the rule's implementation and began interpreting "waters of the United States" consistent with the pre-Clean Water Rule regulatory regime.[58] Meanwhile, under the new Biden administration, and pursuant to President Biden's January 20, 2021, Executive Order on Protecting Public Health and the Environment and Restoring Science to Tackle the Climate Crisis,[59] EPA and the Corps announced that they would initiate a new rulemaking process that first restores the 1986/1988 regulatory definition and then "develops a new rule to establish a durable definition of 'waters of the United States.'"[60] In December 2021, EPA and the Corps proposed a rule that would interpret "waters of the United States" largely in accordance with the 1986/1988 regulatory definition, but would include amendments "to reflect the agencies' interpretation of the statutory limits on the scope of the 'waters of the United States' informed by Supreme Court decisions."[61] The agencies' new rulemaking process will take time, require a substantial record, and almost surely be challenged.

Notwithstanding the rulemaking activity underway, in January 2022, the U.S. Supreme Court granted certiorari in yet another case involving the definition of "waters of the United States."[62] In this instance, the Court will be revisiting the *Sackett* case discussed earlier, this time on the merits. Applying Justice Kennedy's

---

56. *Id.* at 22,251–52.

57. Pascua Yaqui Tribe v. EPA, 2021 WL 3855977, __ F. Supp. 3d __ (D. Ariz. Aug. 30, 2021).

58. *See Current Implementation of Waters of the United States*, EPA, https://www.epa.gov/wotus/current-implementation-waters-united-states (last updated Dec. 20, 2021).

59. 86 Fed. Reg. 7037 (Jan. 20, 2021).

60. *See Revising the Definition of "Waters of the United States,"* EPA, https://www.epa.gov/wotus/intention-revise-definition-waters-united-states (last visited July 1, 2021).

61. 86 Fed. Reg. 69,372, 69,394 (Dec. 7, 2021).

62. Sackett v. EPA, 142 S. Ct. 896 (U.S. 2022).

significant nexus text from his concurring opinion in *Rapanos*, the Ninth Circuit Court of Appeals upheld EPA's exercise of CWA jurisdiction over wetlands on petitioners' property. The Ninth Circuit found that the record supported EPA's conclusion that the wetlands are "adjacent to a jurisdictional tributary and that, together with [a] similarly situated" nearby larger body of wetlands, "they have a significant nexus to" a lake that is a "traditional navigable water."[63] The Supreme Court granted certiorari on the question whether the Ninth Circuit applied "the proper test" for determining CWA jurisdiction. A decision is expected during the Supreme Court's 2022–2023 term.

The scope of federal jurisdiction and definition of "waters of the United States" remains perhaps the most significant and unresolved issue under the CWA. The issue will continue to remain in flux at least until there is another Supreme Court decision resolving it or Congress takes definitive legislative action and amends the statute.

3.2.4 Point Source

"Point source" is defined as "any discernible, confined and discrete conveyance" "from which pollutants are or may be discharged."[64] Examples include a pipe, ditch, channel, tunnel, conduit, well, discrete fissure, container, rolling stock, concentrated animal feeding operation, or vessel or other floating craft.[65] By law, agricultural stormwater discharges and return flows from irrigated agriculture are not "point sources."[66] The cases interpreting the term "point source" have tended to apply the term broadly to include, for example, military aircraft that dropped bombs into the ocean during military training operations[67] and a trap shooting range from which lead shot was fired into waters.[68]

But there are limits to the expansive interpretation of "point source," as evidenced by a controversial ruling that a human being is not a point source and, therefore, that a person who had personally dumped medical waste into the Hudson River could

63. Sackett v. EPA, 8 F.4th 1075 (9th Cir. 2021).
64. CWA § 502(14), 33 U.S.C. § 1362(14); *accord* 40 C.F.R. § 122.2.
65. CWA § 502(14), 33 U.S.C. § 1362(14).
66. *Id.*
67. *See* Weinberger v. Romero-Barcelo, 456 U.S. 305 (1982).
68. Stone v. Naperville Park Dist., 38 F. Supp. 2d 651 (N.D. Ill. 1999).

not be prosecuted under the CWA.[69] The Supreme Court also construed the term "point source" in the *Miccosukee Tribe* case, and rejected the argument that a "point source" must itself be the "source" of the pollution. It noted that "point source" is defined in terms of a "conveyance," which "makes plain that a point source need not be the original source of the pollutant; it need only convey the pollutant to navigable waters."[70]

As mentioned earlier, one type of source included in the definition of "point source" is a concentrated animal feeding operation (CAFO). The Ninth Circuit has held that a dairy's manure storage fields and ditches are part of the CAFO, and are considered point sources under the CWA.[71] The definition of what qualifies as a CAFO is a technical one,[72] and is important given the amount of water pollution that can be produced by such operations. An animal feeding operation is a facility where animals are confined at least 45 days per year and where there is not sustained vegetation (so as to exclude ranches).[73] To be a "concentrated" animal feeding operation, the facility must have a minimum number of animals, with the minimum depending on the type of animal.[74] For example, the threshold number for a "Large CAFO" is 1,000 for slaughter cattle, 700 for dairy cattle, 2,500 for swine, and 55,000 for turkeys.[75]

---

69. United States v. Plaza Health Labs., Inc., 3 F.3d 643 (2d Cir. 1993), *cert. denied*, 512 U.S. 1245 (1994). This decision was vigorously criticized both in the dissent in that case, 3 F.3d at 650, and by subsequent commentators. *See, e.g.*, Ann M. Babigian, *Medical Waste, a Loaded Gun on the Verge of Firing:* United States v. Plaza Health Laboratories, Inc., 13 Pace Env't L. Rev. 1063 (1996). Moreover, *Plaza Health* was a criminal case, which caused the court to construe the Act in a manner more favorable to the defendant than it would have in a civil case.

70. S. Fla. Water Mgmt. Dist. v. Miccosukee Tribe, 541 U.S. 95, 105 (2004); *see also* Decker v. Nw. Env't Def. Ctr., 568 U.S. 597 (2013) (upholding EPA's interpretation of its Industrial Stormwater Rule as permissibly exempting discharges of channeled stormwater runoff from logging roads as point sources requiring an NPDES permit).

71. *See* Cmty. Ass'n for Restoration of the Env't v. Henry Bosma Dairy, 305 F.3d 943 (9th Cir. 2002). The regulation of CAFOs and a rule promulgated by EPA with respect to CAFOs were addressed extensively in *Waterkeeper Alliance, Inc. v. EPA*, 399 F.3d 486 (2d Cir. 2005), which invalidated portions of the rule.

72. *See* 40 C.F.R. pts. 122, 123.

73. 40 C.F.R. § 122.23(b)(1).

74. *Id.* § 122.23(b)(2), (4), (6).

75. *See id.* § 122.23. There are lower thresholds (e.g., 16,500 turkeys) for "Medium CAFOs." *See id.* As a result of these definitions, animal feeding operations are often established at levels that keep them from being a point source and thus requiring a permit.

Several courts have considered whether the fumigant "drift" from the spraying of insecticides and pesticides into or near waters is a discharge from a point source that requires a National Pollutant Discharge Elimination System (NPDES) permit. In *League of Wilderness Defenders v. Forsgren*,[76] the Ninth Circuit held that aerial spraying of insecticides into surface waters constituted a discharge of a pollutant from a point source. In *No Spray Coalition, Inc. v. City of New York*,[77] the federal district court for the Southern District of New York held that helicopters and trucks used by New York City to spray insecticides that reached navigable waters could constitute point sources.

3.3 Discharges to Navigable Waters through Groundwater

Discharges directly into groundwater from a point source are not covered by the CWA since groundwater is not within the scope of navigable waters,[78] and, until recently, courts had been split on whether the CWA applies to point source discharges to groundwater where the groundwater has a direct hydrological connection to navigable waters such as surface waters. In 2020, however, the Supreme Court in *County of Maui v. Hawaii Wildlife Fund* considered the question of "whether the Act 'requires a permit when pollutants originate from a point source but are conveyed to navigable waters by a nonpoint source,' here, 'groundwater.'"[79] The Court held that the CWA applies to discharges to groundwater "if the addition of the pollutants through groundwater is the functional equivalent of a direct discharge from the point source into navigable waters."[80] The Court identified a nonexclusive list of seven factors to determine "functional equivalen[cy]," giving presumptive predominance to the first two factors:

> (1) transit time, (2) distance traveled, (3) the nature of the material through which the pollutant travels, (4) the extent to which the pol-

76. 309 F.3d 1181 (9th Cir. 2002).
77. 2005 WL 1354041 (S.D.N.Y. June 7, 2005).
78. *See* Exxon Corp. v. Train, 554 F.2d 1310, 1329 (5th Cir. 1977).
79. 140 S. Ct. 1462 (2020).
80. *Id.* at 1468.

> lutant is diluted or chemically changed as it travels, (5) the amount of pollutant entering the navigable waters relative to the amount of the pollutant that leaves the point source, (6) the manner by or area in which the pollutant enters the navigable waters, [and] (7) the degree to which the pollution (at that point) has maintained its specific identity.[81]

In early January 2021, EPA issued a Guidance Memorandum on applying the *Maui* "functional equivalen[cy]" test, taking a narrow view of when an NPDES permit is required under the Court's seven factors and adding an eighth factor: "the design and performance of the system or facility from which the pollutant is released."[82] Under the Biden administration, EPA rescinded the Guidance, finding that the eighth factor introduced an intent element that was not consistent with the *Maui* decision.[83] In its memo rescinding the Guidance, EPA stated that it was evaluating appropriate next steps and that in the interim the *Maui* decision would provide the "guiding principles" regarding whether a discharge to groundwater was jurisdictional.

3.4 Exceptions to the Prohibition

Because of the sweeping definitions of section 301's key terms, the exceptions to its prohibition—the authorizations to discharge—are key to compliance with the CWA. By far the most commonly used authorization is that found in section 402, which allows the discharge of certain pollutants under circumstances prescribed by a NPDES permit issued by appropriate state or federal authorities. This authorization is discussed in the next four chapters.

The other most common authorization is that found in section 404, which allows for the discharge of dredged or fill material into navigable waters, including wetlands. This exception is discussed in Chapter 8.

---

81. *Id.* at 1476–77.

82. *See* Anna Wildeman, EPA, Applying the Supreme Court's *County of Maui v. Hawaii Wildlife Fund* Decision in the Clean Water Act Section 402 National Pollutant Discharge Elimination System Permit Program (2021), https://www.federalregister.gov/documents/2021/01/21/2021-01254/applying-the-supreme-courts-county-of-maui-v-hawaii-wildlife-fund-decision-in-the-clean-water-act.

83. 86 Fed. Reg. 53,653 (Sept. 28, 2021).

4 National Pollutant Discharge Elimination System (NPDES) Overview

4.1 The NPDES Process

In drafting the Clean Water Act (CWA), Congress recognized that a blanket prohibition on all water discharges would bring necessary societal activities to a grinding halt. Thus, Congress established a series of exceptions to the prohibition, the most prominent of which is the authorization of a discharge through a permitting process known as the NPDES. Specifically, section 402 of the CWA requires dischargers to obtain a permit before discharging pollutants into "waters of the United States" and establishes procedures for issuing these permits. These permits control pollution by tailoring general pollution control standards to specific facilities and bodies of water.

The NPDES process focuses on two types of direct dischargers, that is, those who deposit pollutants directly into a receiving water body: (1) municipal dischargers, or publicly owned treatment works (POTWs) that receive primarily sewage from residential and commercial customers; and (2) industrial dischargers. Indirect dischargers (those who send wastewater to a direct discharger) are not regulated under the NPDES process but rather are covered by the national pretreatment program, discussed in Chapter 7. For example, those discharging pollutants into a municipal sanitary sewer system do not need NPDES permits, but may be subject to pretreatment requirements. Those discharging into a municipal *storm* sewer system may need an NPDES permit, depending on the type of discharge.

4.2 Exceptions to the NPDES Process

Certain discharges of pollution that might appear to be point sources are specifically exempted from NPDES coverage. For example, discharges governed by section 404 of the CWA (dredged or fill material) and on-site discharges related to cleanups under the Comprehensive Environmental Response, Compensation, and Liability Act[1] are not subject to the NPDES requirement.[2] NPDES permits also are not required for discharges to publicly or privately owned treatment works with their own NPDES permits,[3] or from any return flows from irrigated agricultural activities.[4]

1. 42 U.S.C. §§ 9601 *et seq.*
2. *See* CWA § 404, 33 U.S.C. § 1344; 40 C.F.R. § 122.3(b).
3. *See* 40 C.F.R. § 122.3(c), (g).
4. *See* CWA § 502(14), 33 U.S.C. § 1362(14); 40 C.F.R. § 122.3(f). One longstanding NPDES regulatory exception for discharges incidental to the operation of a vessel, including "sewage from vessels, effluent from properly functioning marine engines, laundry, shower and galley sink wastes" was struck down in 2008 when the Ninth Circuit in *Northwest Environmental Advocates v. U.S. EPA* affirmed a district court decision vacating the exception, finding that it was not authorized by the CWA. 537 F.3d 1006 (9th Cir. 2008). In response to the court's decision, the U.S. Environmental Protection Agency (EPA) in December 2008 promulgated a vessel general permit (VGP) to cover incidental discharges previously exempted from the NPDES process. *See* 73 Fed. Reg. 79,473 (Dec. 29, 2008). The 2008 VGP included, among other provisions, general effluent limitations applicable to all discharges, general effluent limitations applicable to 26 specific discharge streams, and narrative water quality–based effluent limitations. EPA issued a new VGP in 2013 that included numeric technology-based effluent standards for ballast water as well as some changes to the VGP's standards for non-ballast water discharges. 78 Fed. Reg. 21,938 (Apr. 12, 2013). In 2015, the Second Circuit found that EPA acted arbitrarily and capriciously when it issued the 2013 VGP but left the permit in place while EPA responded to the court's decision. Natural Res. Def. Council v. U.S. EPA, 804 F.3d 149 (2d Cir. 2015). The Vessel Incidental Discharge Act of 2018 (VIDA), however, set a new course for regulation of vessel discharges, directing that the 2013 VGP remain in effect without modification until EPA and the U.S. Coast Guard promulgate new standards and related regulations. Pub. L. No. 115-282, §§ 901–903, 132 Stat. 4192, 4322–64.

4.3 NPDES Administration

4.3.1 Levels of State Participation

The NPDES program is managed by the EPA in partnership with state environmental agencies (as well as territories or tribes).[5] States can elect to participate in the NPDES program in three ways. First, a state may simply decline to participate, in which case facilities physically located within that state apply for an NPDES permit from the appropriate EPA regional administrator. Most states do not choose this option because they want the federal funding for environmental protection programs that comes with having an approved state permit program governing discharges to waters, and because they want some say in how the waters within their borders are protected and how in-state dischargers are regulated. Second, a state may seek responsibility for the "base program," issuing base NPDES permits for individual industrial facilities and POTWs. Third, a state capable of issuing base permits can apply for authorization to administer other elements of the NPDES program. These elements include pretreatment, regulation of federal facilities, general permits, and the biosolids (sewage sludge) programs. EPA maintains a web page disclosing which level of authority each state and U.S. territory has been granted.[6] As of June 2021, EPA has authorized 47 states and the U.S. Virgin Islands to implement the base NPDES program.[7]

---

5. As used in this book, the term "state" includes U.S. territories and federally recognized Indian tribes.

6. *National Pollutant Discharge Elimination System (NPDES), NPDES State Program Authority*, EPA, https://www.epa.gov/npdes/npdes-state-program-authority (last visited June 24, 2021).

7. Although they implement the bulk of the base NPDES program within their respective jurisdictions, Oklahoma and Texas are not presently authorized to issue NPDES permits for activities associated with the exploration, development, or production of oil or gas. EPA is the permitting authority for those activities. *See generally NPDES State Program Authority*, *supra* note 6. On June 5, 2018, EPA approved Idaho's application to administer and enforce the full NPDES permit program. Transfer of these functions from EPA to the State is expected to occur over a four-year period in accordance with the Memorandum of Agreement between EPA and Idaho. 83 Fed. Reg. 27,769 (June 14, 2018).

4.3.2 EPA Approval of State Programs

Congress and EPA have established strict requirements for approving state programs. Both the CWA and the EPA's implementing regulations contain provisions establishing the minimum standards.[8] For a state to obtain approval to run a program, it must, among other things:

- Describe the program, including the organization and structure of the organization that will implement it;[9]
- Submit the permit forms, application forms, and reporting forms the state intends to use;[10]
- Describe the state's compliance tracking and enforcement programs;[11]
- Submit a statement from the state attorney general that the state has adequate legal authority to carry out the program;[12]
- Submit a memorandum of agreement between the director of the state agency that will implement the program and the EPA regional administrator, containing provisions for coordination between the state and EPA and for EPA review of state activities;[13]
- Have legal authority to implement EPA's regulations;[14]
- Have specified remedies for enforcement against violators, including suing for injunctive relief to stop violators and to recover civil penalties and criminal fines;[15]
- Provide for judicial review of permit decisions;[16] and
- Have authority to control disposal of pollutants into wells[17] (even though EPA itself does not have such authority under the CWA).

In 1987, Congress amended the CWA to allow EPA to treat eligible federally recognized Indian tribes in a similar manner as

8. *See* CWA § 304(i), 33 U.S.C. § 1314(i); 40 C.F.R. pt. 123.
9. 40 C.F.R. § 123.22(b).
10. *Id.* § 123.22(d).
11. *Id.* § 123.22(e).
12. *Id.* § 123.23.
13. *Id.* § 123.24.
14. *Id.* § 123.25.
15. *Id.* § 123.27.
16. *Id.* § 123.30.
17. *Id.* § 123.28.

a state by adding section 518(e).[18] Currently, there are no federally recognized tribes that have been approved to administer the NPDES program.

As discussed below, even in the states that are authorized to issue NPDES permits, EPA retains oversight authority over state permit decisions, as well as independent enforcement authority.

4.3.3 EPA Power of Review of State Water Quality Standards and Individual Permits

EPA reviews and approves state standards for NPDES permits under section 303(c) of the CWA and 40 C.F.R. part 131.[19] States have primary responsibility for developing standards for waters within their borders, but must review and update these standards every three years to ensure state compliance with current EPA regulations.[20] Additionally, states must examine every three years any water body or segment that does not exhibit water quality consistent with uses specified in section 102(a)(2) of the CWA (i.e., "water quality which provides for the protection and propagation of fish, shellfish, and wildlife and provides for recreation in and on the water") to determine if those uses are feasible.[21] If the uses are feasible, the state must revise its standards accordingly.[22] Reviews also feature public notice and hearings, which are required for any proposed revision of a state water quality standard.[23] If the new state regulations do not conform to the CWA, EPA must promulgate federal water quality standards to replace the state standards.

Subject to waivers and memoranda of agreement between the EPA regional administrator and a state, EPA has veto power over state permits that fail to meet the NPDES standards. The regulations detail the grounds on and procedures by which EPA may object to a permit.[24] The grounds for objection include that the permit "fails to apply, or to ensure compliance with, any applicable" regulatory requirement or that the procedures used materially

18. *See also* 40 C.F.R. § 130.16; 81 Fed. Reg. 65,901 (Sept. 26, 2016).
19. *See* CWA § 303(c), 33 U.S.C. § 1313(c); 40 C.F.R. § 123.44.
20. *See* CWA § 303(c)(1), 33 U.S.C. § 1313(c)(1).
21. 40 C.F.R. § 131.20(a).
22. *See id.* § 131.20(a).
23. *See id.* § 131.20(b). Detailed requirements for such reviews are contained in CWA § 303(c)(2), 33 U.S.C. § 1313(c)(2), and 40 C.F.R. §§ 131.5 and 131.6.
24. 40 C.F.R. § 123.44(c).

failed to comply with statutory or regulatory requirements or memoranda of agreement with EPA.[25] If EPA objects to a permit, EPA must notify the state within 90 days after it receives the proposed permit of the reasons for the objection(s) and the actions the state can take to eliminate the objections. The state then has 90 days to respond to the objections, and may request a public hearing before EPA.[26] After reviewing the state's response and after any public hearing, EPA may reaffirm, modify, or withdraw its objections.[27] Once EPA's disapproval becomes final, authority to issue the permit passes to EPA.[28]

4.4 Applying for a Permit

A discharger seeking an NPDES permit usually approaches the state environmental agency that has been delegated the authority as an "approved state program" under the CWA.[29] In the few states without an approved program, dischargers must obtain a permit from the EPA regional administrator. Once the discharger submits a complete application, a permit writer applies the appropriate standards to the facility at issue.

4.4.1 The Application Process

A "pre-application" conference is often the difference between a complete application that efficiently advances through the process and a series of deficiency notices that delay the proposed project. Applicants should contact the state agency or EPA to request such a meeting, which provides an opportunity for the permitting authority to learn about the project and to provide guidance on what information is needed for a complete application. Regardless of whether there is a pre-application conference, an applicant formally initiates the NPDES permit process by submitting an application to the relevant state official (in states that have EPA-approved programs) or the regional EPA office

25. *Id.* § 123.44(c)(1).
26. *Id.* § 123.44(e).
27. *See id.* § 123.44(g).
28. *See id.* § 123.44(h)(3).
29. CWA § 402(j), 33 U.S.C. § 1342(j).

(in those that do not). Once that official receives the completed application, he or she must decide either to reject it or to prepare a draft permit.[30] If the application is deemed complete, the permitting authority must prepare the draft permit and distribute it to the applicant and interested parties, along with a fact sheet that sets forth "the principal facts and the significant factual, legal, methodological, and policy questions considered in preparing the draft permit."[31] This notice also includes instructions for submitting public comments and requesting a public hearing. The public comment period is both an opportunity and a limitation; parties intending to contest the permit must raise all "reasonably ascertainable issues" to preserve them for consideration on appeal.[32] After the public comment period closes, the permitting authority must make a final permit decision. The permitting authority must then send the decision to all parties that submitted comments and inform them of the procedures for contesting the decision.

4.4.2 Individual Permits

An individual permit is one specifically tailored to a particular facility. The permitting authority develops a permit for that facility based on information contained in the application, and issues the permit for a specific time period (up to five years). The facility must reapply for the permit prior to the expiration date.

4.4.3 General Permits

A general permit covers multiple facilities or activities with similar discharges within a specific category, located in a defined geographical area. General permits may offer both the permittees and the permitting authority a cost-effective option because of the large number of facilities that can be covered by a single permit. To determine whether a general permit is warranted, EPA or the relevant state authority considers the number of facilities to be covered and the similarity of their production processes and pollutants. A discharger seeking to be covered under a general permit issued to another applicant must submit a notice of such intent to the permitting authority.[33] EPA maintains a database

30. 40 C.F.R. § 124.6.
31. *Id.* § 124.8(a).
32. *See id.* § 124.13.
33. *Id.* § 122.28(b)(2).

that allows users to review basic information about facilities that have obtained coverage under most of the more commonly used general permits, including the 2008 and 2012 Construction General Permit, 2008 Multi-Sector General Permit, 2011 and 2016 Pesticide General Permit, and 2008 and 2013 Vessels General Permit.[34]

States that may issue NPDES permits must be specifically authorized to issue general permits.[35] States have issued general permits for a wide range of facilities and/or activities. Before applying for an individual NPDES permit, potential dischargers should determine whether they are eligible for coverage under an authorized general permit.

4.5 Elements of a Permit

4.5.1 Effluent Limitations

The permit writer derives effluent limitations for facilities based on technological and water quality standards. Effluent limitations, which are discussed in detail in Chapters 5 and 6, are the mechanism used to control pollutants in wastewater discharges. Permit writers base effluent limitations in part on the nature of the pollutant involved. In general, there are three categories of pollutants: conventional, toxic, and nonconventional.[36] Conventional pollutants are the main source of concern in the permitting of POTWs. Toxic or priority[37] pollutants pose special risks to human

---

34. *See NPDES eNOI Search Tools*, EPA, https://ofmpub.epa.gov/apex/aps/f?p=LANDING:HOME. This database allows users to search for discharger-specific information.

35. *See* 40 C.F.R. §§ 123.23(c), 123.25(a)(11).

36. CWA section 304(a)(4) designates the following as "conventional" pollutants: biochemical oxygen demand (BOD5), total suspended solids (TSS), fecal coliform, pH, and any additional pollutants EPA defines as conventional. EPA designated "oil and grease" as a conventional pollutant in 1979 (*see* 44 Fed. Reg. 44,501 (July 30, 1979)). "Toxic pollutants" are identified in CWA section 307(a)(1) and listed at 40 C.F.R. § 401.15 and include 126 metals and manmade organic compounds. "Nonconventional" pollutants are those that are neither toxic nor conventional and include parameters such as chlorine, ammonia, nitrogen, phosphorus, chemical oxygen demand, and whole effluent toxicity.

37. EPA derived a more "usable" and "practical" list of priority pollutants from the list of toxic pollutants, which contains open-ended groups of pollutants. The list of priority pollutants identifies chemicals by their individual chemical names. See *Toxic and Priority Pollutants Under the Clean Water Act*, EPA, https://www

health and are more likely to trigger water quality–based effluent limitations. In recent years, nonconventional pollutants such as nutrients (ammonia, nitrogen, phosphorus) have received more attention, and technology improvements at POTWs have enabled additional nonconventional pollutant reduction.[38]

Effluent limitations for NPDES permits are developed in a multistage process. First, the permit writer considers technology-based effluent limitations for each pollutant based either on pre-existing industry standards or on a facility-specific basis. Then, the permit writer consults the state water quality–based effluent limitations (WQBELs) to determine how much a particular facility could discharge into the receiving water without violating water quality standards. The more stringent effluent limitation is then applied in the NPDES permit.[39] A permit may contain different types of limitations for different pollutants. For example, a mercury discharge may be subject to a water quality–based effluent limitation, while phosphate restrictions may be based on a technological limitation. In other words, the limitations on mercury would be developed without regard to economic feasibility, while the permit writer would derive the phosphate restriction by consulting the best practices of similarly situated industries. In all cases, the permit writer documents the decision-making process in the permit fact sheet.

4.5.2 Monitoring and Reporting Requirements

In addition to effluent limitations, the NPDES permit also establishes monitoring and reporting requirements. These requirements allow permanent documentation of waste stream and receiving water conditions. They are the principal means of determining compliance with the permit. Dischargers must monitor themselves by submitting regular discharge monitoring reports. The permit identifies the pollutant parameters that must be sampled, when sampling must occur, the frequency of sampling, the type

.epa.gov/eg/toxic-and-priority-pollutants-under-clean-water-act (last updated Aug. 24, 2020).

38. *See* EPA, EPA-833-B-11-001, Introduction to the National Pretreatment Program (June 2011).

39. The permit writer applies the tougher standard because the CWA sets both "floors" and "goals" for pollution control. Water quality–based standards reflect the idea that the discharge should not reduce the quality of any body of water beneath a certain floor. Technology-based effluent limitations reflect the CWA's goal of eventually eliminating all discharges of pollutants to waters.

of samples that must be taken (grab or composite), the applicable analytical method to be used, and the frequency at which sampling results must be reported. NPDES permits also require prompt reporting of certain types of permit exceedances.[40]

4.5.3 Standard Conditions

EPA requires permits to include several standard requirements for dischargers.[41] These conditions establish standard legal and administrative methods of implementing and complying with the requirements discussed earlier. For example, permittees must maintain and operate treatment equipment at all relevant times, and must allow the representatives of environmental agencies access to the premises for inspection and sampling. Permits may allow a polluter time to install the required equipment; if so, the permit must include the compliance schedule, which generally should not exceed the life of the permit.

The permit must specify its expiration date; permits can last up to five years.[42] However, under the Administrative Procedure Act (APA),[43] a permit issued by EPA will be viewed as fully effective beyond its expiration date if the permittee has timely filed a complete renewal application. This APA extension generally lasts until EPA has taken action on the renewal.[44] For permits issued by authorized states, whether an expired permit continues pending consideration of a renewal is a function of state law. State law typically provides for such continuations.

4.5.4 Special Conditions

If particular "best practices" are not adequately reflected in the effluent limitations, they can be integrated into the permit in the special conditions section. For example, the permit might require a toxicity reduction evaluation: a site-specific study to identify and isolate the causes of effluent toxicity and to evaluate the effectiveness of toxicity controls.

40. 40 C.F.R. § 122.41.
41. *See id.* §§ 122.41, 122.42.
42. *See id.* § 122.46.
43. 5 U.S.C. § 558(c).
44. *See* 40 C.F.R. § 122.6.

4.6 Section 401 Water Quality Certifications

One important feature of the "cooperative federalism" of the CWA is the limitation on a federal agency's authority to issue an NPDES permit, or any other federal permit or license to conduct any activity that may result in a discharge, unless the state in the which the discharge would originate issues or waives a section 401 water quality certification.[45] States can deny certification, or grant certification with conditions, for any federal permit or license that would result in a violation of an applicable effluent standard, water quality criteria, new source performance standard, toxic pollutants restriction, or other state water quality requirement.

States must establish procedures for public notice and hearings regarding applications for 401 certifications. The CWA provides that states must act on a request for a section 401 certification "within a reasonable period of time (which shall not to exceed one year) after receipt."[46] A certifying authority may waive certification expressly, or by failing or refusing to act within a reasonable period of time.[47] The perceived failure of some states to timely review federally permitted energy development and transmission projects requiring section 401 certifications led EPA to overhaul the federal rules governing section 401 in 2020.[48] The relevant federal rules had been largely unchanged since the 1970s, and the revised rule allows federal agencies to establish a reasonable period of time for states to act "either categorically or on a case-by-case basis."[49] Almost immediately, a coalition of states filed a lawsuit in the U.S. District Court for the Northern District of California challenging EPA's revised rule. Then, on

45. CWA § 401, 33 U.S.C. § 1341. *See also* 40 C.F.R. § 121.

46. CWA § 401(a)(1), 33 U.S.C. § 1341(a)(1).

47. *See, e.g.,* N.Y. Dep't of Env't. Conservation v. Fed. Energy Regulatory Comm'n, 991 F.3d 439 (2d Cir. 2021) (upholding the Federal Energy Regulatory Commission's determination that the New York State Department of Environmental Conservation waived its certification authority for a pipeline project despite agreement with applicant to extend one-year time limit); Hoopa Valley Tribe v. Fed. Energy Regulatory Comm'n, 913 F.3d 1099, 1104 (D.C. Cir. 2019) (state impermissibly circumvented the one-year time limit by entering into an agreement with an applicant to repeatedly withdraw and resubmit the application).

48. 85 Fed. Reg. 42,210 (July 13, 2020).

49. 40 C.F.R. § 121.6(a).

May 27, 2021, EPA announced its intent to revise the section 401 certification rule to strengthen the authority of states to protect vital water resources.[50] Both the legal challenge and EPA's rule-making were ongoing as of July 2021.

4.7 Review of Permit Decisions

When an NPDES permit is issued, or a permit application is denied, an affected party may seek review of that decision. This affected party can be the applicant if the permit is denied or, even if the permit is issued, if the applicant believes the permit conditions are overly stringent. An environmental group or citizens who believe the proposed permit is not stringent enough can also be an affected party.

The procedure for seeking review of an NPDES permit varies by whether the permit is issued by EPA or by an authorized state. A party appealing the EPA administrator's issuance or denial of an NPDES permit must first file, within 30 days after EPA's decision, a petition review with EPA's Environmental Appeals Board (EAB) setting forth the basis for the appeal.[51] Such a petition may be filed only by someone "who filed comments on the draft permit or participated in a public hearing."[52] The EAB must decide whether to grant or deny review within a reasonable time after filing.[53] The regulations provide for EAB review only if either a "finding of fact or conclusion of law . . . is clearly erroneous," or the permit reflects an "exercise of discretion or an important policy consideration that the Environmental Appeals Board should, in its discretion, review."[54]

After a decision by the EAB denying review or upholding the permit upon review, the regional administrator must issue the final permit decision.[55] Once the regional administrator has

---

50. 86 Fed. Reg. 29,541 (June 2, 2021). The period for stakeholders to comment on this notice was still open when this publication went to press and it remains to be seen how EPA will revise this controversial rule.
51. *See* 40 C.F.R. § 124.19.
52. *Id.*
53. *See id.*
54. *Id.* § 124.19(a)(4)(i).
55. *See id.* § 124.19(l)(2).

issued a final decision on an NPDES permit after EAB review (or after completion of any remand proceedings after EAB review), a petition for review of the permit can then be filed within 120 days in the U.S. Court of Appeals for the appropriate circuit.[56]

If a person requests EAB review of a decision on a reissued permit, the terms of the reissued permit that are being challenged are stayed, and the terms of the existing permit remain in effect until the EAB review is complete.[57] Any provisions that are uncontested become effective unless they are not severable from the contested provisions.

There is no administrative appeal process and no exhaustion requirement to challenge a federally issued general permit.[58] Under section 509(b)(1) of the CWA, a party must challenge a general permit directly in the U.S. Courts of Appeal, or a party subject to a general permit may apply for an individual permit and appeal the issuance, denial, or conditions of that permit through the process just described.[59]

For permits issued by states authorized to implement the NPDES program, judicial appeals are governed by state law. To obtain NPDES program authorization, however, a state must provide for judicial review of permit decisions. The authorization regulations provide that

> States that administer or seek to administer a program under this part shall provide an opportunity for judicial review in State Court of the final approval or denial of permits by the State that is sufficient to provide for, encourage, and assist public participation in the permitting process.[60]

The judicial review provision cannot restrict the right of either the permittee or persons with affected property or pecuniary interests to seek such review.[61]

---

56. CWA § 509(b)(1), 33 U.S.C. § 1369(b)(1).
57. 40 C.F.R. § 124.16(a).
58. *See id.* § 124.19(a).
59. Section 509(b)(1) of the CWA, 33 U.S.C. § 1369(b)(1), and the question of whether certain challenges must be filed in federal district courts or federal courts of appeals, has been hotly debated as part of the "waters of the United States" controversy discussed in chapter 3. *See generally* Nat'l Ass'n of Mfrs. v. Dep't of Def., 138 S. Ct. 617 (2018).
60. *See* 40 C.F.R. § 123.30.
61. The requirement for state judicial review does not apply to authorized Indian tribes. *Id.*

5 Technology-Based Standards

5.1 Introduction

The 1972 Amendments to the Clean Water Act (CWA) prohibit almost any discharge of pollutants from a point source to waters of the United States, except as authorized by a National Pollutant Discharge Elimination System (NPDES) permit. This was a significant departure from historical efforts to legislate improvements to water quality, which tended to tolerate some pollution. To implement this new approach, the CWA established two primary ways by which discharge limits for these new permits are set. This chapter examines technology-based effluent limitations. The next chapter discusses water quality–based effluent limitations that are established where technology-based effluent limitations are insufficient to meet applicable water quality standards. Technology-based effluent limitations in NPDES permits are derived from national effluent limitations guidelines and new source performance standards promulgated by the U.S. Environmental Protection Agency (EPA) for various categories of point sources (such as industrial, commercial, and public sources). For dischargers in categories for which EPA has not promulgated an applicable national effluent limit or new source performance standard, technology-based effluent limitations are based on the best professional judgment of the permitting authority.

The CWA is technology-focused;[1] thus, it requires consideration of pollution-reducing alternatives available to dischargers.[2] Developing these technology-based standards posed new problems for regulators. Nearly any industrial process could be rendered less polluting—but how much cleaner should it be? On the one hand, a blanket requirement that industry simply use the best technology could impose impossible economic burdens on dischargers. On the other hand, mandating any particular kind of technology could create a disincentive to develop new, more efficient methods of reducing pollution.

To balance these concerns, EPA developed technology-based standards based on the "top performers" in the relevant industry, to be determined by reference to Standard Industrial Classifications (SICs).[3] EPA then sets effluent limitations based on the performance achieved by these top performers. Rather than forcing any particular technology, EPA allowed dischargers to select their means of reducing discharge levels to those achieved by the "best" technologies available at the time. In choosing this approach, EPA sought to establish effluent limits at feasible levels without stifling innovation.

The actual process of setting technology-based standards to be included in individual permits is complex because of the variety of different standards and approaches applied by EPA, all with associated acronyms. Thus, it is helpful to approach the issue in three steps:

1. How high a bar should be set for the technology? Should the best technology available be required of everyone, or is merely good, widely-used technology sufficient?

---

1. *See, e.g.*, Pronsolino v. Nastri, 291 F.3d 1123, 1126 (9th Cir. 2002) ("The 1972 Act therefore sought to target primarily 'the preventable causes of pollution,' by emphasizing the use of technological controls."). Water quality–based standards are instead a "backstop" of regulation, requiring lower effluent limits when existing technology standards fail to maintain water quality at acceptable levels. Water quality–based controls are discussed in Chapter 6.

2. NRDC v. Costle, 568 F.3d 1369 (D.C. Cir. 1977).

3. The Office of Management and Budget replaced the SIC code system with the North American Industrial Classification System developed by the U.S. Census Bureau and this occasionally causes some confusion. EPA guidance on converting these codes, albeit from a non-CWA program, can be found at https://www.epa.gov/toxics-release-inventory-tri-program/tri-covered-industry-sectors.

2. Once it is determined how high the bar will be set, how should guidelines be set and permits be written to ensure that individual facilities achieve the bar?
3. What happens in the event that an individual facility cannot reasonably meet the standards?

5.2 The Range of Technology-Based Standards

Both the nature of the source and the types of pollutants discharged determine the type of technology standards applicable to a permit. Existing sources are subject to (1) the best practicable control technology currently available (BPT) standard, or the average of the best existing performance by well-operated plants within each industrial category or subcategory;[4] (2) the best available technology economically achievable (BAT) standard, or the very best control and treatment measures that have been or are capable of being achieved; or (3) the best available conventional pollutant control technology (BCT) standard, which lies between BPT and BAT. Controls of conventional pollutants[5] are required to meet BPT or, possibly, as discussed in Section 5.2.2 in this chapter, BCT. Controls of toxic and nonconventional pollutants must meet the more stringent BAT.[6] New sources must achieve new source performance standards (NSPS), or "the greatest degree of effluent reduction . . . achievable through application of the best available demonstrated control technology, processes, operating

4. EPA Office of Wastewater Mgmt., NPDES Permit Writers' Manual 5-15, 5-16 (Sept. 2010).

5. CWA section 304(a)(4) designates the following as "conventional" pollutants: biochemical oxygen demand (BOD5), total suspended solids (TSS), fecal coliform, pH, and any additional pollutants EPA defines as conventional. EPA designated "oil and grease" as a conventional pollutant in 1979. *See* 44 Fed. Reg. 44,501 (July 30, 1979).

6. "Toxic pollutants" are identified in CWA § 307(a)(1) and listed at 40 C.F.R. § 401.15 and include 126 metals and man-made organic compounds. "Nonconventional" pollutants are those that are neither toxic nor conventional and include parameters such as chlorine, ammonia, nitrogen, phosphorus, chemical oxygen demand, and whole effluent toxicity.

methods or other alternatives."[7] NSPS are at least as stringent as the BAT, and often more so.[8]

While each of these standards gives some consideration to economic factors, the weight given to such factors should diminish over time. As one court explained, "[a]lthough the EPA is permitted to consider a technology's cost in determining whether it is 'practicable,' 'economically achievable,' or 'available,' it should give decreasing weight to expense as facilities have time to plan ahead to meet tougher restrictions."[9]

5.2.1 Best Practicable Control Technology Currently Available (BPT)

Existing sources are required to utilize at least the BPT standard, the least-exacting standard. To determine BPT, EPA typically "identifies a model technology used by a group of the best performers in an industry, and then sets limits based on the capabilities of that technology."[10] For example, if all of the best-performing companies in a given industry use a specific filter, EPA might require all companies in that industry either to use the filter or to find alternative technologies that reduce pollutants in the discharge at least as much as the filter does. EPA seeks to average the best performances of facilities within the industry, grouped to reflect various ages, sizes, processes, or other common characteristics. Where no company in an industry has adequate technology, EPA may identify technologies in other industries that are transferable.[11]

BPT standards are subject to limited cost-benefit balancing: in setting BPT, consideration is given to "the total cost of application of technology in relation to the effluent reduction benefits to be achieved from such application."[12] Section 304(b)(1)(B) of the CWA provides that the following factors also should be considered in establishing BPT limits: (1) the age of the equipment and

7. CWA § 306(a)(1), 33 U.S.C. § 1316(a)(1).

8. *See, e.g.*, Am. Iron & Steel Inst. v. EPA, 526 F.2d 1027, 1058 (3d Cir. 1975).

9. Riverkeeper, Inc. v. EPA, 358 F.3d 174, 185 (2d Cir. 2004).

10. *See* Legislative History of the FWPCA of 1972, S. Rep. No. 2770, at 169–70 (Oct. 4, 1972) (Conf. Rep.) ("The Administrator should establish a range of 'best practicable' levels based upon the average of the best existing performance by plants of various sizes, ages, and unit processes within each industrial category.").

11. *See* Am. Meat Inst. v. EPA, 526 F.2d 442, 453 (7th Cir. 1975); Tanners' Council of Am. v. Train, 540 F.2d 1188, 1192 (4th Cir. 1976).

12. CWA § 304(b)(1)(B), 33 U.S.C. § 1314(b)(1)(B).

facilities involved; (2) the process employed; (3) the engineering aspects of the application of various types of control techniques; (4) process changes; (5) non-water quality environmental impacts (including energy requirements); and (6) such other factors as the EPA administrator deems appropriate.[13]

5.2.2 Best Conventional Pollutant Control Technology (BCT)

The more stringent BCT may apply to existing facilities that discharge conventional pollutants. BAT is the highest performance in the industry, and can include a higher level of pollution control than is currently being achieved based on technology transferred from a different industrial categories or even foreign facilities. As discussed in Chapter 2, when Congress enacted the 1972 amendments, the CWA required the NPDES to include effluent limits based on BPT by 1977, and effluent limits based on BAT by 1983. By 1977, tensions had arisen between the zero-discharge goal of the CWA and rising concerns about the cost of environmental protection. Environmentalists were concerned that the BPT standard could freeze inadequate pollution control methodologies into law, and they successfully persuaded Congress to endorse a higher standard (BCT) in the 1977 Amendments. But Congress also directed EPA to establish BCT limits only if they passed two distinct cost tests, both intended to ensure that private dischargers did not incur higher compliance costs than publicly owned treatment works (POTWs): the "POTW cost-comparison test," and the "industry cost-effectiveness test."

EPA explained its methodology for the POTW cost-comparison test development of BCT limits in 1986.[14] The POTW test is based on a comparison between the cost (per pound) of pollution reduction by the industry in question and the cost of upgrading an average POTW to advanced secondary treatment capabilities. Presently the POTW test benchmark is $0.46 per pound in 1986 dollars.[15]

The industry cost-effectiveness test is a little more complex. To apply it, EPA compares the incremental gain in pollution reduction to the original gain achieved by BPT. More formally, EPA divides "(i) the cost per pound of the extra conventional pollutants removed using the BCT technology instead of BPT by

13. *See id.*
14. *See* 51 Fed. Reg. 24,974 (July 9, 1986).
15. *Id.* at 24,976.

(ii) the cost per pound of conventional pollutants removed using the BPT technology instead of no control."[16] If that ratio is less than 1.29 (i.e., if removing the BCT-eliminated pollutants costs less than 1.29 times as much as removing the BPT-eliminated pollutants), the candidate BCT passes the industry cost-effectiveness test.[17] Because of these cost tests and other regulatory hurdles, BCT levels have rarely been set above BPT levels.

5.2.3 Best Available Technology Economically Achievable (BAT)

Dischargers of toxic and nonconventional pollutants must adopt the BAT standard in order to reduce these discharges. Unlike the BPT standard, which is based on the average of the best-performing plants, BAT is based on the best of the best-performing plants: EPA models BAT on "the optimally operating plant, the pilot plant which acts as a beacon to show what is possible."[18] This "optimally operating" plant may be foreign and/or a pilot operation.[19] Statutory factors that EPA must consider in assessing BAT include costs, age of equipment and facilities involved, the process employed, potential process changes, non-water quality environmental impacts (including energy requirements), and such other factors as the administrator deems appropriate.[20] EPA has considerable discretion when evaluating BAT, but the statute requires that EPA not impose standards that are "not economically achievable." In making this determination, EPA is required to consider such impacts as potential job losses and plant closings.[21]

5.2.4 New Source Performance Standards (NSPS)

While existing sources of pollution generally are required to add some type of pollution control system at the end of their production process, the CWA requires new sources to integrate pollution-reduction technology into the process itself. Because these

---

16. *Id.*

17. *Id.* Like the POTW test, the ratio of 1.29 is based on the ratio between the cost (per pound of pollutant removed) of upgrading the average POTW from secondary to advanced treatment, and the cost (per pound of pollutant removed) of upgrading from no control to secondary treatment.

18. Kennecott v. EPA, 780 F.2d 445, 448 (4th Cir. 1985).

19. *See* Am. Paper Inst. v. Train, 539 F.2d 328, 353 (D.C. Cir. 1976); Am. Frozen Food Inst. v. Train, 539 F.2d 107, 132 (D.C. Cir. 1976) (foreign plants).

20. CWA § 304(b)(2)(B), 33 U.S.C. § 1314(b)(2)(B); Texas Oil & Gas Ass'n v. EPA, 161 F.3d 923, 928 (5th Cir. 1998).

21. CWA §§ 301(b)(2)(A), 304(b)(2)(B), 33 U.S.C. §§ 1311(b)(2)(A), 1314(b)(2)(B); *see* Am. Petroleum Inst. v. EPA, 661 F.2d 340, 355 (5th Cir. 1981).

sources are new, Congress determined that they could better incorporate the most efficient processes and treatment systems into the design of the facility.[22] Thus, regardless of the type of pollutants they discharge, section 306(b)(1)(B) requires new sources to achieve NSPS.[23]

A "new source" is defined as a source whose construction commenced after relevant performance guidelines were published. "New" refers not only to the time a facility is built but also to the time when EPA promulgated applicable guidelines for that industry. According to the relevant regulations, a new source is any "building, structure, facility or installation . . . the construction of which is commenced . . . [a]fter promulgation of standards of performance under Section 306 of the CWA which are applicable to such source."[24] Therefore, a facility could be a new source for pollutants whose guidelines had been established before construction commenced and an existing source for pollutants covered by guidelines promulgated afterward.

The NSPS are required to reflect "the greatest degree of effluent reduction . . . achievable through application of the best available demonstrated control technologies, processes, operating methods of or other alternatives."[25] This "best available demonstrated technology" (BADT) standard is a strict standard roughly equivalent to the highest achievable effluent reduction,[26] and is at least as stringent as BAT.[27] When establishing NSPS, the CWA directs EPA to consider the cost of achieving the effluent reduction and any non-water quality environmental impacts and energy requirements.[28]

---

22. The Clean Water Act Handbook 23 (2d ed. 2003).

23. New "sources" and new "dischargers" are generally subjected to the same NPDES program requirements as existing sources/dischargers, and section 511(c) of the CWA, 33 U.S.C. § 1371(c), exempts most EPA actions under the CWA from the requirements of National Environmental Policy Act, 42 U.S.C. § 4321 *et seq.* (NEPA). However, CWA section 511(c)(2), 33 U.S.C. § 1371(c)(2), provides that the issuance of NPDES permits for new sources is subject to NEPA. Thus, prior to issuing a NPDES permit to a new source, EPA must determine whether issuing the permit constitutes a "major federal action significantly affecting the quality of the human environment" triggering the need for an environmental impact statement. *See* 40 C.F.R. § 122.21(k) for a list of requirements for NPDES applications from new sources.

24. *See* 40 C.F.R. § 122.2; *see also* CWA § 306(a)(2), 33 U.S.C. § 1316(a)(2).

25. CWA § 314(b)(1)(A), 33 U.S.C. § 1316(b)(1)(A).

26. CWA § 306(a)(1), 33 U.S.C. § 1316(a)(1).

27. *See* Am. Iron & Steel Inst. v. EPA, 526 F.2d 1027, 1048 (3d Cir. 1975).

28. CWA § 306(b)(1)(B), 33 U.S.C. § 1316(b)(1)(B).

5.3 Setting Effluent Limits

Although the CWA envisioned some tailoring of standards to individual plants, it would be impossible for EPA to make case-by-case determinations for the tens of thousands of facilities requiring permits. Pursuant to section 304(b) of the CWA,[29] therefore, EPA has developed general standards for allowable levels of discharge, known as effluent limitation guidelines (ELGs), for a range of pollutants in a variety of industries. The Supreme Court upheld EPA's authority to promulgate such rules in 1977.[30] When setting technology-based standards for facilities in industries not yet governed by ELGs, or pollutants not mentioned within the relevant ELG, the permit writer must use his or her best professional judgment (BPJ) to set effluent limits.

5.3.1 Effluent Limitation Guidelines (ELGs)

EPA employs a set process for establishing technology-based standards. Each technology-based standard must reflect ELGs for the relevant industry and apply the appropriate standard: BPT, BCT, or BAT.[31] ELGs are essentially performance-based standards—they set the maximum range of pollution a facility can discharge. But they are based on technology—that is, on the actually existing methods of achieving pollution control. When EPA develops an ELG for a given pollutant within a particular industry, it must gather and statistically analyze extensive information on industry practices.[32] Using this data, it proposes a menu of options for pollution control in the industry, complete with the projected costs and benefits of each option.[33] After drafting such a menu, EPA crafts a selection of options into proposed limits and explains them in the *Federal Register* with supporting documents.[34] Formal

---

29. CWA § 304(b), 33 U.S.C. § 1314(b).

30. *See* E.I. du Pont de Nemours & Co. v. Train, 430 U.S. 112 (1977); *see also* Am. Frozen Food Inst. v. Train, 539 F.2d 107 (D.C. Cir. 1976) ("Effluent limitations issued pursuant to [the Act] are required to be based upon guidelines and, thus, one very logical interpretation of the Act is that it contemplates issuance of the guidelines first and the effluent limitations afterwards.").

31. CWA § 304(b), 33 U.S.C. § 1314(b), provides for issuance of "guidelines" for categories of pollution point sources.

32. *See generally* NPDES Permit Writer's Manual, *supra* note 4, ch. 5.

33. *See id.*

34. This is based on the flowchart in NPDES Permit Writer's Manual (exh. 5-1).

rulemaking, with public notice and comment, follows this publication, and after this administrative process, nearly every ELG is litigated in court.[35]

The ELG process typically takes five years or more to complete. These delays prompted challenges to EPA's pace of issuing guidelines. This litigation has resulted in two extensive consent decrees, requiring EPA to set guidelines by court-supervised deadlines.[36] Partly as a result of this pressure, EPA has established about 60 categories of industrial ELGs, in categories ranging from "Canned and Preserved Fruits and Vegetables Processing" to "Iron and Steel Manufacturing."[37] For each category or subcategory, EPA typically establishes separate effluent limitations for BPT, BAT, BCT, and NSPS.[38]

To apply ELGs to a particular facility, the permit writer first must determine the industrial category applicable to the plant, using the SIC system.[39] After this determination, application of the relevant ELG, with the relevant standard to the plant, is, in most cases, relatively straightforward.

EPA is constantly revising old ELGs and issuing new ones.[40] To determine whether a particular industry has been covered, whether an ELG is being developed for it, and what the standards are for that industry, it is best to consult the EPA website and EPA's current Effluent Guideline Plan.[41]

---

35. These ELGs can be challenged in a court of appeals only within 120 days of their promulgation. *See* CWA § 509(b), 33 U.S.C. § 1369(b).

36. *See* Schedule for Promulgation by EPA of Effluent Guidelines Under § 304(m) Consent Decree in *NRDC v. Reilly*, Civ. No. 89-2980 (D.D.C. Jan. 30, 1992). EPA's present plan (Effluent Guideline Plan 14) was announced on Nov. 1, 2021, at 86 Fed. Reg. 1960. Plan 14 includes an update on EPA's Per- and Polyfluoroalkyl Substances (PFAS) Multi-Industry study. This study may eventually be used to establish PFAS ELGs that could impact dischargers with SIC codes in the organic chemical, airports, rug and textile, pulp and paper, and metal finishing industrial categories. Effluent guidelines are available on EPA's website at http://www.epa.gov/ost/guide/.

37. For a complete list, see 40 C.F.R. pts. 405–476 and NPDES Permit Writers Manual, *supra* note 4, ch. 5, at 5-24.

38. They also contain pretreatment standards, which are discussed in Chapter 7.

39. NPDES Permit Writer's Manual, *supra* note 4, at 5-25.

40. *See generally id.* ch. 5.

41. *See Effluent Guidelines*, EPA, https://www.epa.gov/eg.

5.3.2 Best Professional Judgment (BPJ)

If the facility is not in an industry covered by an ELG, the permit writer must employ his or her best professional judgment.[42] BPJ permits are based on the same factors used to determine ELGs, but given resource constraints are not as extensively researched. BPJ permits, therefore, are subject to administrative challenge in evidentiary hearings on individual permits. If an ELG standard with less stringent limits than those in a BPJ permit is released after the BPJ permit has been written, the permittee may seek to amend its own permit accordingly. But its ability to do so may be limited by the "anti-backsliding" provision of section 402(o) of the CWA.[43] That provision, subject to several exceptions, generally prevents the effluent limitations in a renewed permit from being less stringent than those in an earlier permit.

5.4 "Fundamentally Different Factors" (FDF) Variance

Because individual permit conditions are premised on nationally developed standards, the CWA recognized that there could be situations where those national standards simply did not fit. Therefore, CWA section 301(n)[44] and EPA's regulations allow for so-called FDF variances to be sought for specific dischargers.[45] The Supreme Court has explained that "EPA has developed its FDF variance as a mechanism for ensuring that its necessarily rough-hewn categories do not unfairly burden atypical plants."[46]

In theory, unique conditions might justify more stringent limits for a particular discharger, and the implementing regulations contemplate such a possibility.[47] However, in practice it is dischargers that utilize this process to seek less stringent limits.

---

42. *See* 33 U.S.C. § 1343(a)(1)(B).

43. *See id.* § 1342(o); *see also* Citizens for a Better Env't-Cal. v. Union Oil Co. of Cal., 83 F.3d 1111 (9th Cir. 1996).

44. CWA § 301(n), 33 U.S.C. § 1311(n).

45. 40 C.F.R. §§ 125.30–125.32.

46. Chem. Mfrs. Ass'n v. Nat. Res. Def. Council, 470 U.S. 116, 120 (1985).

47. *See* 40 C.F.R. § 125.30. The regulations allow "any interested person" to seek a variance, *see id.* § 125.30(b), and provide criteria for making a "request for alternatives limits more stringent than required by national limits," *see id.* § 125.31(c).

EPA, in its implementing regulations, describes the process as follows:

> In establishing national limits, EPA takes into account the information it can collect. In some cases, however, data which could affect these national limits as they apply to a particular discharge may not be available or may not be considered during their development. As a result it may be necessary on a case-by-case basis to adjust the national limits, and make them either more or less stringent as they apply to certain dischargers within an industrial category.[48]

A discharger seeking a less stringent standard must show, among other things, that the alternative standard is only as lenient as the "fundamental difference" justifies, that the variance will not interfere with meeting water quality standards, and that compliance with the national standard will result in either "a removal cost wholly out of proportion to the removal costs considered during development of the national limits" or that there will be a non-water quality adverse environmental impact, including to energy requirements, from applying the national standard.[49]

The regulations specify the types of factors that can be considered as fundamentally different. They include the nature and quality of the pollutants in the wastewater, the volume of wastewater, non-water quality environmental and energy impacts of controlling to national standards, physical and engineering aspects of the facility, and the costs of compliance with the required technology.[50]

There are strict deadlines for seeking an FDF variance. A request must be submitted within 180 days after EPA promulgates an ELG,[51] and it must be based on information submitted to EPA during the development of the ELG, unless there was no reasonable opportunity to submit such information.[52] FDF variances are reviewed on a case-by-case basis, and the burden of proof lies with the entity requesting the variance. In practice, such variances are not often granted.

48. *Id.* § 125.30.
49. *Id.* § 125.31(b).
50. *See id.* § 125.31(d).
51. CWA § 301(n)(2), 33 U.S.C. § 1311(n)(2).
52. CWA § 301(n)(1)(B), 33 U.S.C. § 1311(n)(1)(B).

5.5 BAT Variances

In addition to FDF variances, the CWA authorizes EPA to grant variances (1) for economic incapability and (2) with respect to a narrow category of nonconventional pollutants. Section 301(c) provides that EPA may grant variances to dischargers who demonstrate that proposed alternative limits "will represent the maximum use of technology within the economic capability of the owner or operator" and "will result in reasonable further progress toward the elimination of the discharge of pollutants."[53] The variance is not available for any toxic pollutant listed in section 307(a)(1), and the discharger who receives this variance still must comply with BPT limits for the pollutant at issue.[54] The second BAT variance applies only to ammonia, chlorine, color, iron, and phenols.[55] Dischargers must demonstrate that the variance would not interfere with the attainment or maintenance of water quality, result in additional requirements on other point or nonpoint sources, or prevent the discharger from satisfying BPT.[56] EPA rarely grants either type of variance.

53. CWA § 301(c), 33 U.S.C. § 1311(c).
54. CWA § 301(*l*), 33 U.S.C. § 1311(*l*).
55. CWA § 301(g), 33 U.S.C. § 1311(g).
56. CWA § 301(g)(2), 33 U.S.C. § 1311(g)(2).

6 Water Quality–Based Effluent Limitations

6.1 Introduction

If technology-based effluent limits are based on an array of legal standards, cost-benefit evaluations, and engineering judgments concerning pollution-reducing alternatives available to dischargers, numeric water quality–based effluent limitations (WQBELs) are relatively straightforward. WQBELs are based exclusively on the potential that a discharge may cause or contribute to a violation of water quality standards in the receiving waters.[1] And, unlike technology-based limits, WQBELs are applied based on water quality without regard to cost.[2]

Clean Water Act (CWA) section 303(c)(2)(A) requires that water quality standards be established based on the highest and best use of the water body, including use and value for public water supplies; propagation of fish and wildlife; recreation; and agriculture, industry, navigation, and other purposes.[3] WQBELs are developed by the states,[4] with each state designating the uses of its navigable waters and the water quality criteria necessary for such uses and determining the maximum load of each pollutant that the water body can handle without exceeding the identified water quality standard.

1. CWA § 302(a), 33 U.S.C. § 1312(a).
2. Nat. Res. Def. Council v. U.S. EPA, 808 F.3d 556, 565 (2d Cir. 2015).
3. CWA § 303(c)(2)(A), 33 U.S.C. § 1313(c)(2)(A).
4. If a state fails to adopt water quality standards, the administrator must do so for the state. CWA § 303(b), 33 U.S.C. § 1313(b).

6.2 History and Purpose of Water Quality–Based Effluent Limits

WQBELs are intended to provide independent standards for pollution control when technology-based standards are ineffective.[5] Section 303 of the CWA mandates that state or regional officials identify polluted waters, rank them for cleanup, identify the total load of pollution that affected water bodies could safely absorb, and take steps to reduce point and nonpoint source pollution loadings to this level.[6] Despite this mandate, throughout the 1970s and 1980s many of these steps either never occurred or proved ineffective. The U.S. Environmental Protection Agency (EPA) took the position that it had no enforceable duty to act under section 303, claiming that technology-based programs had not yet had a chance to work.[7] Even as federal officials became more receptive to WQBELs, various issues—including the complexity of the relevant science, political opposition, and the difficulty of addressing the role of nonpoint sources—impeded their development. Moreover, because state agencies devoted nearly all of their efforts to the development, application, and enforcement of technology-based standards, by 1999, "only 19 percent of the nation's rivers, lakes, and estuaries [had] been assessed for pollution, and these for, in most cases, only the most rudimentary contaminants."[8]

As a result of regulators' heavy reliance on technology-based standards, by the 1990s, water bodies throughout the United States remained significantly impaired. A 1998 study reported that more than 20,000 water bodies had high pollution levels, including over 300,000 river and shoreline miles and five million acres

5. For an excellent discussion of the history of water quality–based standards, see Oliver A. Houck, The Clean Water Act TMDL Program: Law, Policy, and Implementation (2d ed. 2002).

6. CWA § 303(d), 33 U.S.C. § 1313(d).

7. *See, e.g.*, Env't. Def. Fund v. Costle, 9 Env't. L. Rep. (Env't Law. Inst.) 20,716, 13 Env't Rep. Cas. (BNA) 1867 (D.D.C. 1979), *aff'd*, 657 F.2d 275 (D.C. Cir. 1981).

8. Oliver A. Houck, *TMDLs IV: The Final Frontier*, 29 Env't L. Rep. 10,469, 10,469–70 (1999) (citing TMDL Fed. Advisory Comm. Act Comm., Final Report 3 (May 20, 1998)).

of lakes.[9] By the mid-1990s, citizen suits began to force greater focus on WQBELs.[10]

6.3 Establishing Water Quality–Based Effluent Limits (WQBELs)

As just described, the CWA provides for WQBELs to complement technology-based effluent limits. Determination of WQBELs is a three-step process. First, the state must identify water quality standards for each water body within its jurisdiction. Second, the state must determine the total maximum daily load (TMDL) of certain pollutants that each water body can handle and still meet the water quality standards identified. Third, WQBELs must be imposed on dischargers to the particular water body through their National Pollutant Discharge Elimination System (NPDES) permits.

6.3.1 Determining Water Quality Standards

Section 303(d)(1) of the CWA requires states to identify waters within their borders for which technology-based effluent limitations are not sufficient to achieve any water quality standard applicable to such waters. To this end, the statute requires states to develop water quality–based standards and review those standards every three years.[11] EPA either may approve or reject these standards.[12] Although the CWA requires states to undertake this assessment, financial limitations on state resources often dictate a far less rigorous process of assessing water quality. Focusing on identifying the most polluted waters, states submit a list of these water quality–limited segments (WQLSs) to EPA, along with an

9. EPA, Final TMDL Rule: Fulfilling the Goals of the Clean Water Act (July 2000), https://nepis.epa.gov/EPA/html/DLwait.htm?url=/Exe/ZyPDF.cgi/P10059ZN.PDF?Dockey=P10059ZN.PDF.

10. *See, e.g.*, Raymond Proffitt Found. v. U.S. EPA, 930 F. Supp. 1088 (E.D. Pa. 1996); Columbia River United v. Reilly, 1991 WL 338250 (W.D. Wash. 1991).

11. All states are required by section 303(c) of the Clean Water Act, 33 U.S.C. § 1313, to set state water quality standards for all bodies of water located in the state.

12. To avoid disapproval, states usually follow the procedures mentioned in EPA, Water Quality Standards Handbook (updated Nov. 2017), http://water.epa.gov/scitech/swguidance/standards/handbook/index.cfm. This publication is based on 40 C.F.R. part 131. EPA standards are a floor, not a ceiling; states can develop stricter standards. CWA § 510, 33 U.S.C. § 1370.

account of the level of use they aim to attain.[13] EPA can either approve the list, reject it, or approve it with amendments. The state then must devise a plan for bringing listed WQLSs up to their designated use.[14]

There are three distinct steps to the development of water quality standards. First, states classify the designated "use level" of water bodies. Second, states establish the "water quality criteria" necessary to protect the designated uses for each water body, and determine the maximum effluent that a water body may receive without exceeding the water quality criteria. Third, states must ensure compliance with the state's antidegradation policy.

6.3.1.1 Use Classifications

Section 303(c) of the CWA requires states to designate uses for all water bodies within their borders.[15] Designated uses include, at minimum, existing uses, but may also reflect higher levels of potential use.[16] Common uses include public water supply; recreational, agricultural, and industrial uses; and propagation of fish and wildlife. States may designate several compatible uses for the same body of water.[17] States also have designated more specific classifications relating to agricultural and aquacultural objectives. Although states retain discretion in their choice of classification, the general "fishable/swimmable" goal of section 101(a)(2) of the CWA controls where feasible. If a state sets designated uses below the fishable/swimmable level, it must demonstrate through a use attainability analysis that attainment of that level is not feasible. Specifically, the state must comprehensively assess the physical, chemical, biological, and economic factors affecting achievement of the designated use. The state must show that one of six

13. A complete list of WQLSs in each state is available at *Clean Water Act Section 303(d): Impaired Waters and Total Maximum Daily Loads (TMDLs)*, EPA, https://www.epa.gov/tmdl (last visited June 30, 2021), and the WQLSs (along with parameters of concern) are displayed graphically (and charted for some states). The procedural details of the state-listing process are discussed in EPA Office of Wastewater Mgmt., NPDES Permit Writers' Manual (Sept. 2010), https://www.epa.gov/sites/production/files/2015-09/documents/pwm_2010.pdf.

14. After the list has been drawn up, states are entitled to set priorities among the listed water bodies.

15. EPA, Introduction to Water Quality Standards 5 (Oct. 1999), https://nepis.epa.gov/EPA/html/DLwait.htm?url=/Exe/ZyPDF.cgi/20003TCA.PDF?Dockey=20003TCA.PDF.

16. Existing uses include all uses that have been attained since November 28, 1975. *See* 40 C.F.R. § 131.3(e).

17. CWA § 303(c), 33 U.S.C. § 1313(c).

specified conditions prevails in order to set designated uses below the fishable/swimmable goal. These conditions include that the use is prevented by such things as naturally occurring pollution, low flows, or irremediable human-caused conditions, or that more stringent controls "would result in substantial and widespread economic and social impact."[18]

6.3.1.2 Water Quality Criteria

As a necessary complement to these intended use levels, states must also establish water quality criteria necessary to protect designated uses.[19] These criteria describe the quality of the water body. There are three approaches to water quality criteria: (1) numeric chemical-specific limits, (2) whole effluent toxicity, and (3) biological assessments.

Numeric chemical-specific limits. Chemical-specific criteria are concentrations of individual pollutants that may enter a body of water based on its uses. This "chemical-specific" approach is perhaps the most direct way to safeguard water quality via WQBELs. If, for instance, a water quality standard for cadmium is established at 4 micrograms per liter (meaning that the levels in the water body should be below that number), the permit writer sets effluent limits such that this pollutant never reaches that particular concentration in the receiving water being addressed. This can be a simple process if there is only one discharger. If there are multiple dischargers and nonpoint sources, setting effluent limits can be difficult to accomplish without a TMDL.

Whole effluent toxicity (WET). The WET approach assesses the impact of the interactions between all the chemicals within the effluent on organisms in the receiving water. WET is defined as the "aggregate toxic effect of an effluent measured directly by a toxicity test."[20] It measures the overall toxicity of a discharger through its effect on aquatic organisms. WET limits can look to acute effects—what concentration of effluent kills 50 percent of exposed test organisms in two days—or chronic effects, such as impaired reproduction over a longer exposure. The goal of this approach is to require the permit holder to ensure that its effluent will not have an observed adverse effect on aquatic life in the

18. *See* 40 C.F.R. 131.10(g).
19. CWA § 303(a)–(c), 33 U.S.C. § 1313 (a)–(c).
20. 40 C.F.R. § 122.2.

receiving water. The use of such a standard is intended to ensure that, even if chemical-specific criteria are met, the overall effluent is not toxic.[21]

Biological assessments. Even the WET approach may not be sufficient to protect water quality; therefore, water quality–based toxics control also employs a biological assessment approach.[22] This approach is used to assess the overall biological integrity of an aquatic community.[23] State environmental officials first catalog the members of an aquatic community and determine their ecological role.[24] They then compare this survey to a reference waterbody with a similar designated aquatic life use.[25]

In addition to these quantitative criteria, which specify the precise concentration of pollutants permitted, EPA allows states to use so-called narrative criteria, which are often used to protect the aesthetics and health of a water body and can be expressed in lay terms. For example, state water quality criteria may require that water be "free of objectionable color, odor, taste, and turbidity." Most states, eager to avoid expensive monitoring and scientific risk assessments, have preferred narrative to numeric criteria. Responding to this in 1987, Congress required the states to develop numeric criteria for the toxic pollutants listed pursuant to section 307. EPA has also prioritized technical assistance and support in this area in order to make generally available the science behind numeric criteria.

Dischargers and applicants seeking permits who find themselves subject to WQBELs often resort to schedules of compliance, variances, site-specific criteria, seasonal limits, or mixing zones that may be allowed in state permit programs. When a discharger is unable to immediately comply with WQBEL, the

21. *See generally Permit Limits-Whole Effluent Toxicity (WET)*, EPA, https://www.epa.gov/npdes/permit-limits-whole-effluent-toxicity-wet (last visited July 14, 2021). In December 2004, EPA issued draft guidance for the use of WET limitations in the NPDES process. *See* EPA, National Whole Effluent Toxicity (WET) Implementation Guidance Under the NPDES Program (2004), http://www.epa.gov/npdes/pubs/wet_draft_guidance.pdf.

22. This is also known as a bioassessment or biocriteria approach.

23. .EPA, Primer on Using Biological Assessments to Support Water Quality Management 1 (Oct. 2011), https://www.epa.gov/sites/production/files/2018-10/documents/primer-using-biological-assessments.pdf.

24. EPA, Biological Criteria: National Program Guidance for Surface Waters (Apr. 1990), https://www.epa.gov/sites/production/files/2018-10/documents/national-program-guidance-surface_waters.pdf.

25. NPDES Permit Writers' Manual, *supra* note 13, at 6-12.

NPDES permit can include a "schedule of compliance" allowing compliance over time.[26] A variance offers temporary relief from an effluent limit but not permanent reclassification of the receiving water and must include conditions to ensure that the permittee makes reasonable progress toward achieving the WQBELs.[27] Site-specific criteria can be applied in locations where local water chemistry differs significantly from the water chemistry that the state relied on when developing the criteria (but are exceedingly difficult to apply to WQBELs).[28] Finally, it may be possible to negotiate seasonal permit limits that allow increased loading of a particular pollutant when natural conditions are favorable or a mixing zone where initial dilution of a discharge is permitted. These techniques are not limited to NPDES permits featuring WQBELs, but because WQBELs often present the most challenging and expensive compliance issues in a NPDES permit, these compliance alternatives often arise in connection with permits that include WQBELs.

6.3.1.3 Antidegradation Policy

While the most ambitious goal of the CWA (elimination of all discharges) is not presently the focus of EPA's permitting program, EPA nevertheless is committed to stopping any avoidable loss of water quality. Thus, each state is required to adopt an antidegradation policy consistent with EPA's antidegradation regulations.[29] The regulations require that state policy accomplish, at a minimum, three things. For all waters, "existing instream water uses and the level of water quality necessary to protect the existing uses shall be maintained and protected."[30] For higher-quality waters, where "the quality of the waters exceeds levels necessary to support the protection and propagation of fish, shellfish, and wildlife and recreation," that higher quality must be "maintained and protected" unless the state finds after a full and open process that "allowing lower water quality is necessary to accommodate

26. *See generally* 40 C.F.R. §131.15. *See also* Catskill Mountains Chapter of Trout Unlimited, Inc. v. U.S. EPA, 846 F.3d 492, 519 (2d Cir. 2017).

27. Variances are authorized by 50 C.F.R. § 131.14.

28. *See* EPA Water Quality Standards Handbook, *supra* note 12, at ch. 3, § 3.5.2, at 15.

29. 40 C.F.R. § 131.12. This regulation also requires states to publish the specific methods they will use in order to implement their policy.

30. *Id.* § 131.12(a)(1).

important economic or social development in the area in which the waters are located."[31] For the highest-quality waters that constitute an outstanding national resource (like those in national and state parks and wildlife refuges), that water quality must be maintained and protected without exception.[32] If a discharge is proposed that could degrade existing higher-quality water, there must be an opportunity for public participation and intergovernmental coordination in the decision to allow or deny the proposed activity. If the public response, taken as a whole, is opposition to the activity, the state cannot allow the activity without a substantial and convincing justification.[33]

6.3.2 Total Maximum Daily Loads (TMDLs)

Although states have considerable latitude in devising plans to meet water quality standards, section 303(d) of the CWA and its implementing regulations require states to estimate the TMDL of pollutants that an impaired water body can receive and still attain its designated uses.[34] TMDLs must be established for each pollutant that prevents a water body from reaching water quality standards. The process of establishing TMDLs is highly technical, and states typically retain consultants to develop and analyze the relevant data. EPA, comparatively speaking, has a relatively limited role in the TMDL process, as section 303(d) provides only that EPA has authority to approve or disapprove a state's TMDL list or submittal, and to prepare a list or submittal in the event it disapproves of the state's list or submittal.[35] The allocation must

31. *Id.* § 131.12(a)(2).

32. *Id.* § 131.12(a)(3).

33. *See* Clean Water Act Handbook 32 (Mark A. Ryan ed., 2d ed. 2003).

34. For additional information regarding procedures for developing water quality standards, refer to EPA's Water Quality Standards Regulations at 40 C.F.R. part 131 and the EPA Water Quality Standards Handbook. According to EPA, more than 40,000 TMDLs have been completed. By far the most complex TMDL involves the Chesapeake Bay. This TMDL addresses nitrogen, phosphorus, and sediment quality throughout a 64,000-square-mile watershed that includes portions of Delaware, Maryland, New York, Pennsylvania, Virginia, West Virginia, and the District of Columbia. *See generally Chesapeake Bay TMDL, Frequent Questions About the Chesapeake Bay TMDL*, EPA, https://www.epa.gov/chesapeake-bay-tmdl/frequent-questions-about-chesapeake-bay-tmdl (last visited June 30, 2021).

35. EPA's decision to approve or disapprove a state's section 303(d) lists and TMDLs may be challenged in federal district court under the Administrative Procedure Act as final agency action. The court may set aside EPA's decision if it determines that the decision was arbitrary, capricious, an abuse of discretion, or otherwise contrary to law. *See, e.g.*, Am. Canoe Ass'n v. U.S. EPA, 30 F. Supp. 2d 908, 924 (E.D. Va. 1998).

address both point and nonpoint sources, as well as air deposition and natural background sources.[36] The allocation to a point source is called a wasteload allocation (WLA), and the allocation for nonpoint sources and natural background conditions is called a load allocation. The TMDL must take into account "seasonal variations and a margin of safety."[37] Although section 303(d) describes the loads as "daily," the implementing regulations provide that TMDLs also may be expressed "in terms of either mass per time, toxicity, or other appropriate measure."[38]

The TMDL process is important to integrating point and nonpoint source regulations into a watershed-based approach.[39] Nevertheless, state and federal officials were slow to implement the regulations in earnest, and much of that effort was due to litigation against EPA. In 1996, in response to a number of these lawsuits, EPA began a comprehensive review of the TMDL process that ended in July 2000, when EPA finalized extensive and controversial revisions to the program.[40] The revisions did not take effect, however, because EPA initially delayed the effective date after Congress included a "TMDL rider" in an appropriations bill to bar EPA from expending funds to implement the rule.[41] At the same time, many parties challenged the 2000 rule in court. In October 2001, EPA further delayed the rule's effective date,[42] and in March 2003, EPA formally withdrew the rule.[43]

At present, TMDLs have been set for only a small fraction of impaired waters. A single water body may have impairments from

36. *See* CWA § 303(d)(1)(c), 33 U.S.C. § 1313(d)(1)(C).

37. *Id.* The regulations do not prescribe a specific margin of safety percentage. Rather, this figure is left to EPA's discretion. *See* Nat. Res. Def. Council, Inc. v. Muszynski, 268 F.3d 91 (2d Cir. 2001).

38. 40 C.F.R. § 130.2(i). In *Friends of the Earth v. EPA*, 446 F.3d 140 (D.C. Cir. 2006), the D.C. Circuit held that TMDLs could be expressed only in "daily" terms, finding the language of section 303(d) unambiguous. In response, EPA in November 2006 published guidance confirming its position that, depending on the circumstances, "daily" limits are not always appropriate. *See* Establishing TMDL "Daily" Loads in Light of the Decision by the U.S. Court of Appeals for the D.C. Circuit in *Friends of the Earth, Inc. v. EPA* and Implications for NPDES Permits, EPA Memorandum from Benjamin Grumbles, Assistant Administrator, to Regional Directors (Nov. 15, 2006), https://www.epa.gov/sites/production/files/2015-10/documents/2006_11_21_tmdl_anacostia_memo111506.pdf.

39. The TMDL process was established by Clean Water Act section 303(d), and EPA promulgated regulations at 40 C.F.R. § 130.7.

40. 65 Fed. Reg. 43,585 (July 13, 2000).

41. *See* 65 Fed. Reg. at 43,660.

42. 66 Fed. Reg. 53,043 (Oct. 18, 2000).

43. 68 Fed. Reg. 13,607 (Mar. 19, 2003).

more than one pollutant. Thus, most impairments have yet to be addressed through the TMDL process. Because WLAs constrain WQBELs only where TMDLs have been set, they do not presently influence most water quality–based standard-setting processes.

Once a state has set TMDL standards, it must provide "reasonable assurance" that pollution will eventually decline to the levels prescribed.[44] Such assurance requires reducing pollutant levels for all sources to their WLAs or load allocations. This is much easier for point than nonpoint sources. While TMDL limitations for the former can be folded into NPDES permits, EPA has only recently proposed methods of regulating nonpoint sources.[45]

6.3.3 Threshold Determination of the Need for WQBELs

Given the various tools available for setting WQBELs, the question for a permit applicant is what exactly triggers their application to a particular discharger.

According to EPA regulations and policy, every permit writer must consider the impact of a permit on water quality levels.[46] After applying technology-based limits to a discharger, the permit writer must project whether the pollution allowed by the permit will result in the violation of the water quality criteria for the relevant body of water.[47] If the discharge "causes, has the reasonable potential to cause, or contributes to an in-stream excursion above a narrative or numeric criteria above a State water quality standard," the permit writer must impose a WQBEL that is stricter than the applicable technology standard.[48] The regulations require that when determining whether a particular discharge will cause, or has the reasonable potential to cause, an in-stream excursion above a state water quality standard, the permitting authority shall use procedures that account for various factors that could affect the outcome, including existing controls on point and nonpoint

44. Further guidance related to establishing TMDLs can be found in EPA, Guidance for Water Quality–Based Decisions: The TMDL Process (1991), https://www.epa.gov/sites/production/files/2018-10/documents/guidance-water-tmdl-process.pdf, and EPA, Technical Support Document for Water Quality–Based Toxics Control (1991), http://www.epa.gov/npdes/pubs/owm0264.pdf.

45. *See infra* Chapter 11.

46. NPDES Permit Writers' Manual, *supra* note 13, at 6-1 ("a permit writer must consider the impact of the proposed discharge on the quality of the receiving water").

47. *See* 40 C.F.R. § 122.44(d).

48. *Id.*

sources of pollution and the dilution of the effluent in the receiving water.[49]

If effluent monitoring data are available, the permit writer can employ an analytical method called a mass balance equation to determine the WQBEL. This simplified water quality model assumes steady-state, or constant, conditions for variables such as background pollutant concentrations and stream flow.[50]

Even if effluent monitoring data are lacking, a WQBEL can be derived using alternative data. If the permit writer cannot monitor a plant's effluent precisely and project from that figure, he or she can develop a WQBEL using the "type of industry or POTW [publicly owned treatment works], existing data on toxic pollutants, history of compliance problems and toxic impact, and type of receiving water and designated use."[51] Such WQBELs must be based on an assessment of the pollutant level that a body of water can sustain, and also on projections from the response of similar bodies of water to similar pollution stresses.

6.4 Water Quality Trading Policy of 2003

On January 13, 2003, EPA issued a Water Quality Trading Policy that endorses the implementation of water quality trading programs for nutrients, sediments, and other pollutants, and provides guidance and encouragement for the development and implementation by states, interstate agencies, and tribes of such programs.[52] The program does not apply to trading with respect

49. *See id.*

50. NPDES Permit Writers' Manual, *supra* note 13, at 6-15.

51. EPA, U.S. EPA NPDES Permit Writers' Manual 103 (Dec. 1996), https://nepis.epa.gov/EPA/html/DLwait.htm?url=/Exe/ZyPDF.cgi/20004BM3.PDF?Dockey=20004BM3.PDF. In addition, CWA section 304(l) addresses the challenges presented by toxic pollutants and reflects Congress's conclusion that use of the best available technology economically achievable would not always be sufficient to control toxic pollutants. Section 304(l) creates a mechanism for states and EPA to identify impaired waters in which technology-based effluent limitations have proven insufficient. In these locations, states must develop and continuously refine individual control strategies requiring permits issued to point sources in those waters to include supplemental water quality-based effluent limitations. 33 U.S.C. § 1314(l)(1).

52. *See* EPA, Water Quality Trading Policy, *in* Water Quality Trading Toolkit for Permit Writers, app. B (June 2009), https://www.epa.gov/sites/production/files/2016-04/documents/wqtradingtoolkit_app_b_trading_policy.pdf.

to technology-based limits. The policy essentially "allows one source to meet its regulatory obligations by using pollutant reductions created by another source that has lower pollution control costs."[53] Its purpose is to capitalize on market-based approaches to achieve greater water quality and environmental benefits than would otherwise be achieved through traditional approaches.[54] It is focused on the trading of nutrient loads (such as total phosphorus and total nitrogen) or sediment loads.[55] Proposed trades of other pollutants may be acceptable but require a higher level of scrutiny.[56] Cross-pollutant trading may also be acceptable for pollutants that deplete oxygen, where adequate information exists to establish and correlate impacts on water quality.[57] The trading of persistent bioaccumulative toxics, however, is not allowed.[58]

On February 6, 2019, EPA issued a memorandum reiterating its support for market-based mechanisms, including water quality trading,[59] and on September 19, 2019, EPA published a *Federal Register* notice inviting the public to consider and comment on policy options that could help promote market-based approaches to water quality improvements.[60] Water quality trading is also discussed in Chapter 11.

Whatever the potential for EPA's trading policy to provide flexibility and lower costs, this program has yet to show significant results, and its fate remains unclear.

---

53. *Id.* at B-2.
54. *See id.*
55. *See id.* § III.C.
56. *See id.*
57. *See id.*
58. *See id.*
59. *See* Updating the Environmental Protection Agency's (EPA) Water Quality Trading Policy to Promote Market-Based Mechanisms for Improving Water Quality, EPA Memorandum from David P. Ross, Assistant Administrator, to Regional Administrators (Feb. 6, 2019), https://www.epa.gov/sites/production/files/2019-02/documents/trading-policy-memo-2019.pdf.
60. 84 Fed. Reg. 49,293 (Sept. 19, 2019).

7 Regulations of Publicly Owned Treatment Works and Pretreatment Requirement for Dischargers to Publicly Owned Treated Works

7.1 Introduction

Whereas Chapters 5 and 6 focus on *direct* industrial dischargers, this chapter addresses two other significant sources of water pollution: (1) publicly owned treatment works (POTWs)[1] and (2) industrial users that send their waste to POTWs, known as *indirect* dischargers. POTWs and indirect dischargers are subject to different standards than direct industrial dischargers. POTWs are responsible for treating wastewater, and must purify it in several ways before discharging. Indirect dischargers are not required to obtain National Pollutant Discharge Elimination System (NPDES) permits, but may be required to obtain a permit by the POTW,

1. "Publicly owned treatment works" is defined in the regulations as a treatment works owned by a state or municipality. 40 C.F.R. § 403.3(q). Section 212 of the Clean Water Act defines "treatment works." *See* 33 U.S.C. § 1292.

and must comply with both national "categorical" and "local" pretreatment requirements.

As of 2012, there were approximately 15,000 POTWs in the United States, responsible for treating more than 40 billion gallons of wastewater each day, and serving more than 75 percent of the U.S. population.[2] POTWs are often difficult to regulate because of their unique dual role in the water quality improvement regime: they are both polluters and treaters of pollution, both regulators and regulated bodies. While the U.S. Environmental Protection Agency (EPA) could seek to shut down a private discharger that repeatedly and recalcitrantly violated its NPDES permit, shutting down a POTW would be counterproductive to the goals of the Clean Water Act (CWA) because there is no means to stop or redirect a POTW's collection system. Thus, because even a noncompliant POTW usually is better than one that has been shut down,[3] EPA approaches POTW regulation differently than it does industrial dischargers.

While POTWs are required to follow a number of federally mandated prescriptions, EPA traditionally has supplemented these requirements with a number of incentives. One of the most important incentives has been funding for improved or innovative treatment programs through the Clean Water State Revolving Fund (CWSRF) program, which uses a combination of federal and state funds to provide loans for construction of municipal wastewater facilities and decentralized wastewater treatment facilities, among other infrastructure projects.[4] Capitalized by the federal and state governments,[5] the CWSRF program is a method for the federal government to provide seed money for innovation, while

2. EPA, EPA-830-R-15005, CLEAN WATERSHEDS NEEDS SURVEY 2012: REPORT TO CONGRESS 25 (Jan. 2016) [hereinafter NEEDS SURVEY], https://www.epa.gov/sites/production/files/2015-12/documents/cwns_2012_report_to_congress-508-opt.pdf; *see also* EPA, EPA-833-B-11-001, INTRODUCTION TO THE NATIONAL PRETREATMENT PROGRAM 1-1 (June 2011) [hereinafter PRETREATMENT INTRODUCTION], https://www.epa.gov/sites/default/files/2015-10/documents/pretreatment_program_intro_2011.pdf.

3. As Professor Oliver Houck explains, "The federal leverage over sewer dischargers that are not in compliance is quite limited. Fines against these violators are assessed with increasing frequency, but there are limits to what can be wrung from hard-pressed municipal budgets. Moreover, while an industrial discharge can be enjoined, no one has seriously proposed shutting down a POTW." Oliver Houck, *Ending the War*, 47 MD. L. REV. 358, 380–81 (1988).

4. *See Clean Water State Revolving Fund*, EPA, https://www.epa.gov/cwsrf/learn-about-clean-water-state-revolving-fund-cwsrf (last updated July 3, 2021).

5. Funds to establish or capitalize the CWSRF programs are provided by the federal (80 percent) and state (20 percent) governments. *Id.*

monitoring treatment developments by imposing conditions on the loans. The CWSRF has provided $145 billion to communities through 2020.[6] EPA's Report to Congress on the Clean Watershed Needs Survey 2012 identified $271 billion as the amount of wastewater infrastructure capital investment required to address water quality or water quality-related public health problems (as of 2012).[7]

7.2 Regulation of Discharges from POTWs

POTWs predate modern clean water legislation and are a central feature of modern sanitation. They historically have focused on treating domestic sewage by ridding sewer water of visible pollutants. While POTWs still fulfill this traditional role, they now supplement it with scientifically based efforts to control conventional pollutants and toxics. POTWs must meet water quality-based standards very similar to those applicable to comparable industrial point sources,[8] but must comply with different technology-based limitations, focused on reducing five conventional pollutants: (1) biological oxygen demand (BOD), (2) total suspended solids, (3) fecal coliform, (4) acidity (pH), and (5) oil and grease.[9]

7.2.1 NPDES Permits for POTWs

Permit application requirements for POTWs are set forth at 40 C.F.R. § 122.21(j). The information required varies depending on the size of the POTW (measured by its daily flow rate) but generally includes the population served by the POTW, ownership of the facility, the type of collection system used, effluent monitoring data, and wastewater flow rate.[10] All POTWs must identify whole effluent toxicity tests conducted during the four and a half years preceding the application; larger POTWs also must submit the results of valid tests.[11]

6. *See id.*
7. Needs Survey, *supra* note 2, at 6.
8. *See* 33 U.S.C. § 1311(b)(1)(C).
9. 40 C.F.R. § 122.21(j)(4)(i); 40 C.F.R. pt. 122 app. J tbl. 1A.
10. *See* 40 C.F.R. § 122.21(j)(1).
11. *See id.* § 122.21(j)(5)(i)–(ii).

Section 122.41(m)(1) of the POTW NPDES regulations prohibits "bypassing" or intentionally diverting wastewater from the POTW unless (1) the bypass was necessary to prevent loss of life, injury, or severe property damage; (2) there were no feasible alternatives to bypass; and (3) the permittee submitted required notices.[12]

A number of POTWs experience problems during heavy rains, when flows to the plant exceed capacity. To manage flows during these times, operators route some flow around the secondary treatment units, then recombine, or "blend," the rerouted flow with flows from the secondary treatment facility before disinfecting and discharging. EPA, in December 2005, proposed a rule that would have permitted the practice if a utility completed a "no feasible alternatives" analysis and determined that blending was the only feasible option to handle flows during heavy rains.[13] Although EPA did not finalize the rule, in June 2010 it announced plans to hold several "listening sessions" to obtain public input on the policy and potential modifications to it, but never officially finalized the rule.[14] However, EPA adopted some of the policy's concepts in subsequent letters, which the Eighth Circuit Court of Appeals later held to be a legislative rule promulgated in violation of the Administrative Procedure Act's notice and comment requirements.[15] The court also found that policy conflicted with existing secondary treatment regulations because it applied effluent limitations within facilities' secondary treatment processes, rather than at the final point of discharge into navigable waters.[16] In response to the decision, EPA made statements that it would not follow the decision outside of the Eighth Circuit, but would continue to evaluate blending on a case-by-case basis elsewhere in the country.[17] EPA sought input from public health experts on

12. *See id.* § 122.41(m)(4)(i). In *United States v. City of Toledo*, the U.S. District Court for the Northern District of Ohio held that "no feasible alternative" includes the circumstance in which the POTW could have taken preventive measures to increase plant capacity. 63 F. Supp. 2d 834 (N.D. Ohio 1999).

13. *See* 70 Fed. Reg. 76,013 (Dec. 22, 2005).

14. *See* 75 Fed. Reg. 30,395 (June 1, 2010).

15. Iowa League of Cities v. EPA, 711 F.3d 844, 876 (8th Cir. 2013).

16. *Id.* at 877.

17. *See* Ctr. for Regulatory Reasonableness v. EPA, 849 F.3d 453, 454 (D.C. Cir. 2017), in which industry challenged the EPA's "non-acquiescence statement's legality, including claims that the non-acquiescence statement was itself a rule promulgated without proper notice and comment and in excess of the agency's statutory authority." The D.C. Circuit dismissed the case on jurisdictional grounds.

the implications of blended discharge effluent from sewage treatment in 2014.[18] In 2018, EPA sought comments from the public regarding possible approaches to updating the NPDES regulations pertaining to managing peak wet weather flows, but has not issued any further policies or rules.[19]

7.2.2 Primary Treatment Requirements

Primary treatment of wastewater removes large solids (e.g., rags and debris) and smaller inorganic grit.[20] Several methods contribute to successful primary treatment. For example, a POTW may keep wastewater in a tank, permitting heavier solids to settle and lighter pollutants to rise to the top.[21] Screening and filtration can also eliminate certain solids. Such primary treatment purifies water while leaving behind sewage sludge.

7.2.3 Secondary Treatment Requirements

Even if POTWs perfected primary treatment, wastewater would remain polluted by materials that neither sink nor float. Accordingly, section 301(b)(1)(B) of the Clean Water Act requires effluent limitations for POTWs to be based on secondary treatment, which removes many of these pollutants by "using microorganisms to consume biodegradable organics."[22] Of the five conventional pollutant standards, three—BOD (biological oxygen demand), total suspended solids, and acidity (pH)—are reduced by secondary treatment.[23] Secondary treatment is required to achieve an effluent level below 30 milligrams per liter for both BOD_5 (five-day biological oxygen demand) and total suspended solids, averaged over 30 days.

Since the adoption of the CWA, it has become increasingly apparent that secondary treatment is best achieved by certain types of technologies. As a result, the focus of both the CWA and its implementing regulations has shifted from establishing goals to

18. *See Experts Forum on the Public Health Impacts of Wet Weather Blending*, EPA, https://www.epa.gov/npdes/peak-flows-sewage-treatment-plants (last updated Feb. 4, 2021).

19. *See* 83 Fed. Reg. 44,623 (Aug. 31, 2018).

20. Pretreatment Introduction, *supra* note 2, at 1-1.

21. The latter can be scraped off and left behind as the water is passed to another tank.

22. Pretreatment Introduction, *supra* note 2, at 1-1.

23. EPA's secondary treatment standards set acceptable levels for each of these water quality parameters. *See* 40 C.F.R. § 133.102.

prescribing methods of attaining them. For example, a 1981 legislative amendment expanded the definition of secondary treatment by identifying "biological treatment facilities [such] as oxidation ponds, lagoons, and ditches and trickling filters" as "the equivalent of secondary treatment."[24] Some monitoring requirements are relaxed when POTWs adopt one of the statutorily prescribed methods of secondary treatment.

7.2.4 Tertiary (or Advanced Secondary) Treatment Requirements

If the discharges from a POTW adversely affect a water body even after primary and secondary treatment, the POTW may be required to implement advanced secondary, or tertiary, treatment, which can include processes such as nitrification, denitrification, chemical treatment to remove toxics, and disinfection to kill pathogens.[25] EPA is authorized to require the adoption of tertiary treatment on a case-by-case basis,[26] though it is far more likely to utilize incentives in order to induce adoption of these techniques.

7.2.5 Sewage Sludge Treatment and Biosolid Disposal

Primary, secondary, and tertiary treatments remove from wastewater a residue known as sewage sludge, defined as "any solid, semisolid, or liquid residue removed during the treatment of municipal waste water or domestic sewage."[27] Recent survey data indicate that POTWs generate approximately 13.8 million tons (dry weight) of sludge annually.[28] Section 405 of the CWA[29] governs the use and disposal of sewage sludge, and EPA in 1993 promulgated regulations implementing that provision, published at 40 C.F.R. part 503. Section 405(d) of the CWA requires EPA to establish numeric limits and management practices that protect public health and the environment from reasonably anticipated

---

24. CWA § 304(d)(4), 33 U.S.C. § 1314(d)(4).

25. *See* The Clean Water Act Handbook 95 (Mark A. Ryan ed., 4th ed. 2018).

26. *See* Montgomery Env't. Coal. v. Costle, 646 F.2d 568 (D.C. Cir. 1980).

27. 40 C.F.R. § 501.2.

28. *See* Univ. of Mich. Ctr. for Sustainable Sys., Factsheet: U.S. Wastewater Treatment (2020), https://css.umich.edu/us-wastewater-treatment-factsheet.

29. 33 U.S.C. § 1345. Congress amended section 405(d) in 1987 to direct EPA to set numeric limits to protect public health and the environment from adverse effects of pollutants in sewage sludge. EPA failed to meet the specified timetable for doing so, resulting in a citizen suit, *Gearhart v. Reilly*, No. 89-6266-HO (D. Or. 1989).

adverse effects of chemical and microbial pollutants during the use or disposal of sewage sludge, and to review sewage sludge regulations every two years to identify any additional pollutants that may occur in biosolids, and update them accordingly. And 40 C.F.R. part 503 establishes requirements for the use or disposal of sludge when it is applied to land to condition the soil or fertilize vegetation, disposed of in a municipal landfill or surface disposal site, or fired in a biosolids incinerator.

Biosolids (a term often used interchangeably with "sewage sludge") are a semi-solid, nutrient-rich product created when solids separate from liquids during the wastewater treatment process.[30] Biosolids are divided into "Class A" and "Class B" designations based on treatment methods, pollutant limits, pathogen and vector attraction reduction requirements, and management practices.[31] Class A biosolids cannot contain detectable pathogen levels and must meet vector attraction reduction requirements; Class B biosolids can contain detectable pathogen levels. Over half of biosolids can be beneficially useful after treatment.[32] The most common method for using biosolids is in land application (spreading of biosolids on the soil surface or incorporating it into soil), and is most often used in agriculture, though they can also be applied in reclaiming mine sites and other disturbed lands, as well as in parkland and golf courses.[33]

Land application of biosolids has been the subject of numerous litigations, as neighboring property owners often complain about odors. In 2003, a federal district court found that two Virginia county ordinances, which effectively banned the application of biosolids on agricultural land, were preempted by state laws and declared them void and unenforceable.[34] In a 2009 case, *City of Los Angeles v. County of Kern*, which involved a constitutional challenge by users and transporters of biosolids to Kern County's ban on the import and land application of biosolids,[35] the Ninth Circuit found that the ordinance did not burden the recyclers' interest in the interstate waste market, since nothing in the

30. *Basic Information about Biosolids*, EPA, https://www.epa.gov/biosolids/basic-information-about-biosolids (Mar. 2, 2021).
31. *See* 40 C.F.R. § 503.32.
32. *See* Univ. of Mich. Ctr. for Sustainable Sys., *supra* note 28.
33. *Id.*; *see also Basic Information about Biosolids*, *supra* note 30.
34. O'Brien v. Appomattox Cnty., 293 F. Supp. 2d 660, 667 (W.D. Va. 2003).
35. 581 F.3d 841 (9th Cir. 2009).

measure precluded them from shipping the waste out of state and dismissed the case on prudential standing grounds.[36] However, plaintiffs re-filed in California state court, which in 2017 found that the biosolids ban was preempted by state law and exceeded the county's police power.[37] Similarly, a Washington appeals court found in 2014 that a county ordinance banning the use of the most common class of biosolids was unconstitutional because it irreconcilably conflicted with state laws and regulations providing for disposal and land application of biosolids.[38] And in 2015, the Supreme Court of Pennsylvania examined a case brought by residents of an agricultural area who asserted nuisance claims based on the "unusually noxious" and "extremely offensive" odors emanating from nearby farmland after biosolids were spread on the fields.[39] The court found that the nuisance claims were precluded by the state's Right to Farm Act because land application of biosolids, which is closely regulated by the state, is a "normal agricultural operation" and therefore the farmers were shielded from nuisance claims.[40]

7.3 Regulation of Discharges to POTWs: Pretreatment Standards

As companies that discharged directly to waters under the NPDES program felt the squeeze of technology-based and water quality-based standards, they moved toward discharging to POTWs. As a result, POTWs came under scrutiny for potentially "passing through" pollution that would have been regulated as a point source discharge if it had been discharged to the nearest water

36. *Id.* at 849 ("Because the recyclers' injury is not even 'marginally related' to the interests the [Commerce] Clause seeks to safeguard, they lack prudential standing to bring their federal constitutional claim.").

37. City of Los Angeles v. Cnty. of Kern, No. VCU242057, 2017 WL 1292822, at *31 (Cal. Super. Ct. Mar. 14, 2017).

38. State Dep't of Ecology v. Wahkiakum Cnty., 184 Wash. App. 372, 378, 337 P.3d 364, 367 (Wash. Ct. App. 2014).

39. Gilbert v. Synagro Cent., LLC, 634 Pa. 651, 656, 131 A.3d 1, 3 (2015).

40. *Id.* at 687.

body.[41] EPA developed the pretreatment program to regulate such indirect dischargers.

Pretreatment standards require dischargers to POTWs to eliminate or drastically reduce wastes that would either interfere with the operation of a POTW or pass through the POTW's treatment systems to the receiving water.[42] After some initial litigation, the terms "interference" and "pass through" are now, as described later in the chapter, relatively well defined, providing a foundation for POTW and EPA regulations.[43] The General Pretreatment Regulations require all large POTWs (i.e., those that can treat five million gallons or more of intake per day) and some smaller ones to adopt local pretreatment rules.[44]

The multitiered system of environmental regulation often renders POTWs responsible for enforcing national, state, and local laws and regulations regarding indirect discharge.[45] Just as states apply to develop an NPDES program, they may also apply to be the approval authority responsible for monitoring the POTW pretreatment programs in the state.[46] Regardless of which approval authority directly governs a POTW, the treatment works must implement EPA's minimum pretreatment standards.[47] Both POTW officials and other local authorities can add more ambitious objectives to the national baseline standards.

7.3.1 History of Pretreatment Standards

Congress was aware of the danger of direct dischargers shifting their wastes from point source disposal to POTWs; accordingly,

41. *National Pretreatment Program Overview*, EPA, https://www.epa.gov/npdes/national-pretreatment-program-overview (last updated Aug. 27, 2020).

42. CWA § 307(b)(1), 33 U.S.C. § 1317(b)(1); 40 C.F.R. § 403.2(a), (b).

43. *See* 40 C.F.R. § 403.3.

44. *See id.* § 403.8(a). The rules are designed to prevent pass through and interference, and to eliminate certain toxic pollutants to the greatest extent possible. *See id.* § 403.2. For an overview of the pretreatment rules, see Pretreatment Introduction, *supra* note 2, at 2-2-7.

45. For a comparison of the roles of different officials in the Pretreatment Program, see Pretreatment Introduction, *supra* note 2, at 4-1-2.

46. As of August 2020, only 36 states were certified to regulate their POTW pretreatment programs. *See National Pretreatment Program Implementation*, EPA, https://www.epa.gov/npdes/national-pretreatment-program-implementation (last updated Aug. 27, 2020).

47. This floor of standards mandates that the POTWs possess certain legal authority and funding and maintain certain procedures and reporting systems. Pretreatment Introduction, *supra* note 2, at 2-6 fig. 2-4 (listing the six minimum pretreatment program elements).

Congress required EPA to promulgate a list of pollutants unsuitable for treatment at POTWs that direct dischargers would have to reduce or eliminate before sending wastewater to a POTW. When EPA failed to meet the statutory deadline, litigation led to a consent decree that established deadlines for EPA to set pretreatment limits on many toxic pollutants and to establish guidelines for indirect dischargers.[48] As a result of the decree, EPA promulgated General Pretreatment Regulations in 1978.[49] EPA also committed to developing pretreatment standards applicable to indirect dischargers emitting wastewater contaminated by any of the 129 "priority pollutants," as well as any others deemed incompatible with POTW treatment capacities.[50]

As discussed earlier, POTWs must hold an NPDES permit. In addition to the reporting requirements of a POTW's NPDES permit, EPA requires POTWs themselves to regulate the discharges of their customers. POTWs must have legal authority to monitor and investigate their users, to enforce compliance with pretreatment standards, and to seek or levy fines of $1,000 a day for violations of the standards.[51] EPA regulations require POTWs to focus their efforts on significant industrial users (SIUs). SIUs are those that meet one of four criteria: they discharge over 25,000 gallons a day of process wastewater; they contribute more than 5 percent of the POTW's capacity; they have the capacity to adversely affect the POTW's operation or to violate pretreatment requirements; or they are subject to federal categorical standards (discussed in Section 7.4.2).[52]

---

48. *See* Env't. Def. Fund, Inc. v. Costle, 636 F.2d 1229, 1234 & n.8 (D.C. Cir. 1980), *appeal after remand*, 718 F.2d 1117 (D.C. Cir. 1983), *cert. denied*, 467 U.S. 1219 (1984). This litigation was resolved as part of the comprehensive settlement on toxic discharges, called the Flannery decree, which anticipated the use of technology-based controls covering 21 major industries and 65 specified pollutants or groups of pollutants. Promulgation of the regulations envisioned by the agreement was to take place according to a phased schedule running through 1979 and compliance was to be achieved by 1983. Ridgway M. Hall, Jr., *The Evolution and Implementation of EPA's Regulatory Program to Control the Discharge of Toxic Pollutants to the Nation's Waters*, 10 Nat. Res. Law. 507, 519–20 (1978).

49. Pretreatment Introduction, *supra* note 2, at 2-2.

50. *See id.* Three priority pollutants were removed from the list of priority pollutants in 1981. *Toxic and Priority Pollutants under the Clean Water Act*, EPA, https://www.epa.gov/eg/toxic-and-priority-pollutants-under-clean-water-act (last updated July 10, 2021).

51. 40 C.F.R. § 403.8(f).

52. *Id.* § 403.3(v).

7.3.2 Monitoring/Reporting and Record-Keeping Requirements

Industrial users of POTWs face a number of reporting requirements.[53] All industrial users must notify their POTW immediately if an unexpected event results in discharge that could cause or contribute to problems at the POTW.[54] These discharges are known as "slug loadings;" examples include spills and other accidents. If a POTW determines that certain industrial users are violating pretreatment requirements with episodic overloads, they may require those dischargers to develop a plan to control slug discharges.[55] Industrial users also must notify their POTWs if their discharges change substantially, or suddenly include any material deemed hazardous waste.[56]

Industrial users covered by categorical standards must comply with special reporting requirements. They must monitor their discharge in baseline, compliance, and periodic reports to be filed with both local and federal officials.[57] Local regulators determine the reporting requirements for industrial sources not covered by categorical requirements. Those classified as SIUs must report at least once every six months.[58]

7.3.3 Program Submission and Approval

EPA has two means of assuring that POTWs develop and enforce pretreatment programs. First, many POTWs accept grants from the federal government in order to construct facilities and develop new treatment technologies; these grants are conditioned on the POTW's commitment to develop a pretreatment program. Second, POTWs' NPDES permits include pretreatment requirements that the POTW, in turn, must enforce against its users. To fulfill either obligation, the POTW must be legally capable of monitoring and controlling contributions to the system, conducting inspections, and monitoring and obtaining remedies for noncompliance. The POTW also must demonstrate a realistic plan for financing its activities and finding qualified personnel.[59]

---

53. *See* PRETREATMENT INTRODUCTION, *supra* note 2, at 5-1–5-8.
54. *See* 40 C.F.R. § 403.12(f).
55. *See id.* § 403.8(f)(2)(vi).
56. 40 C.F.R. § 403.12(j), (p)(1). "Hazardous waste" is defined in 40 C.F.R. part 261.
57. *See* 40 C.F.R. § 403.12. For a table listing these and other reporting requirements, see PRETREATMENT INTRODUCTION, *supra* note 2, at 5-13–5-15.
58. *See* 40 C.F.R. § 403.12(h).
59. *See id.* § 403.8(f).

7.4 Substantive Requirements of Pretreatment Program

EPA imposes a number of substantive requirements on the regulation of industrial dischargers by POTWs. All POTWs must enact "local limits" on industrial discharges in order to ensure compliance of the POTW with the POTW's own permit, and with other provisions of the CWA.[60] EPA has adopted some "national pretreatment standards" that are generally applicable (general pretreatment standards) and others that are applicable only to particular types of industries (categorical standards).[61]

7.4.1 General Pretreatment Standards

The CWA mandates pretreatment whenever a wastestream threatens either "pass through" or "interference."[62] "Pass through" occurs when an industrial user of a POTW delivers waste that would cause the POTW to violate its NPDES permit.[63] A discharge "interferes" with the POTW when it so inhibits the POTW's treatment or sewage sludge processes that it causes a violation of the POTW's NPDES permit or prevents its compliance with the statutes and regulations governing sewage sludge disposal.[64] Industrial users must pretreat their discharge if it will likely pass through or interfere with the POTW's treatment process. POTWs usually develop local limits in order to ensure that these events do not occur.[65] Certain substances are banned outright from discharge to POTWs, including discharges that present a fire hazard, corrode the POTW's structures, or generate toxic fumes endangering POTW personnel.[66] Other pollutants are earmarked for special controls, depending on their toxicity and site-specific impact.[67]

7.4.2 Categorical Standards

Just as EPA establishes a variety of technology-based limits on direct discharges, it requires POTWs to set limits on indirect

60. *See id.* § 403.8(f)(4).
61. *See id.* §§ 403.5, 403.6.
62. *See also* Pretreatment Introduction, *supra* note 2, at 1-2.
63. *See* 40 C.F.R. § 403.3(p).
64. *See id.* § 403.3(k).
65. *See id.* § 403.5(c)(1).
66. *See id.* § 403.5(b).
67. *Id.*

discharges based on the best available technology economically achievable (BAT).[68] The standards are tailored to particular industries, such as electroplating, feedlots, textile mills, and battery manufacturing. Industry-based categorical standards ensure that required reductions of discharges are realistic and fair. They also are designed to equate regulation of discharges from all polluters, so that the recovery water is not worse off because a source discharged first to a POTW. Categorical standards essentially are determined by subtracting the amount of pollution eliminated by the POTW from the effluent limitation guideline that would apply if the plant were a direct discharger.[69] There are some variations; EPA considers "non-water-quality environmental impacts, available pollution prevention measures, and economic effects" before promulgating categorical pretreatment standards.[70]

There are two types of categorical pretreatment standards: pretreatment standards for existing sources (PSES) and pretreatment standards for new sources (PSNS). The PSES correspond very closely to the BAT standards applied to similar direct discharges, with some allowances and variances to accommodate the diverse situations and capacities of dischargers.[71] The PSNS govern all structures constructed after the proposal of the applicable PSNS, if such a structure necessitates an entirely new pollution prevention process, or "replaces" an earlier source, or is "substantially independent" from existing sources.[72] The PSNS are similar to the new source performance standards (NSPS) applied to direct dischargers under section 306 of the CWA; they are based on the best available demonstrated control technology standards.[73]

---

68. CWA § 307(b), 33 U.S.C. § 1317(b).

69. *See* Pretreatment Introduction, *supra* note 2, at 3-3.

70. *Id.*

71. *See* 52 Fed. Reg. 42,522, 42,525 (Nov. 5, 1987) (preamble to the final rule for Organic Chemicals and Plastics and Synthetic Fibers Category Effluent Limitations Guidelines, Pretreatment Standards, and New Source Performance Standards). Note, though, that categorical pretreatment standards do not vary on the basis of the size or waste treatment capacity of the POTW to which industrial users are discharging. This inflexibility is designed to ensure that facilities within a regulated industry achieve a nationally uniform degree of pollution control.

72. *See* 40 C.F.R. §§ 122.2, 122.29. "New source" is defined at 40 C.F.R. § 403.3(m).

73. *See* Pretreatment Introduction, *supra* note 2, at 3-5.

7.4.3 Locally Imposed Substantive Standards

EPA's categorical standards are only a baseline and do not preempt local efforts to establish more stringent controls on pollution.[74] Municipalities also deploy a wide variety of enforcement techniques.[75] Local standards are too varied for a simple summary, but they are important.

Although municipalities are an autonomous source of pollution regulations, their agendas increasingly complement or reflect EPA concerns. For example, since EPA scientifically determines safe levels of toxic pollutants, local authorities concentrate on conventional pollutants. Although nearly any POTW is formally capable of reducing conventional pollutants to levels prescribed by its NPDES permit, a POTW may choose to accept only a certain level of conventional pollutant discharge from each indirect discharger. Overloaded POTWs can resort to local standards in order to manage waste flows better.

7.5 POTW Pretreatment Program Variances and Removal Credits

Some indirect dischargers objected to categorical pretreatment standards because their POTWs were already removing the pollutants covered by the categorical standards. These dischargers felt that their POTWs could safely take responsibility for removing such pollutants, and that they should not, in essence, have to pay twice for the same removal. Initially, EPA balked at permitting this shifting of responsibility, but as POTWs became more efficient and sludge management advanced,[76] Congress authorized EPA to permit POTWs to modify the categorical pretreatment standards to take into account the pollutant removal that the POTW consistently achieves. To the extent a POTW "consistently removes" a

74. "Nothing in this subsection shall affect any pretreatment requirement established by any State or local law not in conflict with any pretreatment standard established under this subsection." CWA § 307(b)(4), 33 U.S.C. § 1317(b)(4).

75. *See* Pretreatment Introduction, *supra* note 2, at 4-10.

76. The decision to allow removal credits was intimately linked with the promulgation of sludge management standards. The Water Quality Act of 1987, § 406(e), dictated that POTWs could not grant removal credits until EPA promulgated regulations regarding the disposal of sewage sludge.

certain pollutant, it can grant removal credits to indirect dischargers otherwise required to pretreat their waste for that pollutant.[77] Particularly efficient POTWs may remove so much waste from the effluent received that they entirely eliminate the need for pretreatment of given pollutants.[78]

POTWs may grant a very limited set of variances from categorical pretreatment standards. Just as in the case of technology-based NPDES permitting (discussed in Chapter 5), an affected polluter may apply for a fundamentally different factors variance. To obtain the variance, the facility must demonstrate that it is "fundamentally different" from the facilities that EPA considered when the relevant rule was promulgated.[79] Such variances must be submitted very soon (typically within 180 days) after the facility is affected by EPA rulemaking.[80] One other variance allows plants to adjust assessments of the pollution level in their discharges in accordance with the level of pollution in their intake waters.[81] Facilities are responsible only for their net addition to the pollution level of the water they use.[82]

7.6 Collection System Challenges

A major focus of many POTWs in recent years has been their collection systems (i.e., sewer systems), which bring wastewater to their treatment system. Collection systems present challenges in a number of ways. First, many of the sanitary sewage systems in large U.S. cities are old and deteriorating. If the sewer system does not deliver the wastewater to the POTW, the POTW obviously cannot treat it, and the untreated wastewater can find other paths to reach surface waters or other undesired locations.

A related challenge facing POTWs is the mixing of stormwater in their collection systems. In some cases, that is because the POTW is an older system with a combined sanitary and stormwater collection system. For such systems, wet-weather

77. 40 C.F.R. § 403.7(b).
78. *See* Pretreatment Introduction, *supra* note 2.
79. CWA § 301(n), 33 U.S.C. § 1311(n); 40 C.F.R. § 403.13.
80. 40 C.F.R. § 403.13(g).
81. *See id.* § 403.15.
82. *See id.*

events can overwhelm their treatment capacity. For other systems that have separate sanitary and stormwater collection systems, stormwater frequently infiltrates the sanitary wastewater collection system. These wet-weather challenges are discussed in Chapter 10. Addressing combined sewer overflow systems and sanitary sewer overflows have been an enforcement priority for EPA in recent years, and "keeping raw sewage and contaminated stormwater out of the nation's waters" was identified on EPA's lists of National Enforcement Initiatives for both the 2014–2016 cycle[83] and the 2017–2019 cycle.[84]

83. *See National Enforcement Initiatives for Fiscal Years 2014–2016: Keeping Raw Sewage and Contaminated Stormwater Out of Our Nation's Waters*, EPA, https://www.epa.gov/enforcement/national-enforcement-initiatives-fiscal-years-2014-2016-keeping-raw-sewage-and (last updated Oct. 28, 2020).

84. News Release, EPA, EPA Announces National Enforcement Initiatives for Coming Years (Feb. 18, 2016), https://archive.epa.gov/epa/newsreleases/epa-announces-national-enforcement-initiatives-coming-years.html; *see also* EPA, EPA National Enforcement Initiative: Keeping Raw Sewage and Contaminated Stormwater Out of Our Nation's Waters (May 1, 2017), https://www.epa.gov/sites/production/files/2017-05/documents/epa-nei-css-consent-decree-tracking-table-050117.pdf (identifying 45 civil consent decrees between EPA and municipalities across the country regarding combined sewer overflows).

8 Regulation of Wetlands

8.1 Introduction

Much of the development of the modern-day United States has been enabled by the conversion of swamps, bogs, playas, prairie potholes, marshes, and other aquatic environments now classified as "wetlands" under the Clean Water Act (CWA). For example, in the 17th century, the area that is now the lower 48 states contained an estimated 220 million acres of wetlands,[1] more than half of which have since been drained, dredged, and filled to make way for development.[2] Major metropolises—including Chicago, New Orleans, Miami, and Washington, D.C.—have been built on former swamps, and one could drive for hours past Midwestern farm fields that were once saturated marshes. By the late 20th century, however, as impacts from floods and droughts became more prevalent, and various species of animals and plants slipped away, Americans realized there was an immense cost associated with this development. Although federal law had actively encouraged conversion of wetlands for over a century,[3] by the 1970s, Congress recognized the need to place the force of federal regulation behind preservation of the nation's priceless hydrological and ecological resources.

---

1. *See* Thomas E. Dahl & Gregory J. Allord, *Technical Aspects of Wetlands: History of Wetlands in the Conterminous United States*, *in* National Water Summary on Wetland Resources (U.S. Geological Survey Water Supply Paper 2425, last modified Mar. 1997), http://water.usgs.gov/nwsum/WSP2425/history.html.

2. *See id.*

3. *See id.* (discussing the federal Swamp Land Acts passed between 1849 and 1860).

Thus, as part of the 1972 amendments that form the basis of today's Clean Water Act, Congress elected to protect wetlands by regulating under section 404 the discharge of dredged or fill material into the nation's navigable waterways, interpreted to include adjacent wetlands. If we conceive of section 301 of the CWA as a broad ban on all discharges, section 404 is the portion that dictates the terms for authorization of discharges affecting the *physical structure* and *function* of aquatic ecosystems.[4] The centerpiece of section 404 is a rigorous—and controversial—permitting scheme that requires government review of any proposed project that could result in a discharge into "jurisdictional" wetlands (i.e., wetlands that are "waters of the United States"). In practice, this means that landowners and developers seeking permits are sometimes informed that they may not develop the land at all, or that they must do so in a particular fashion, or that they must compensate for resulting wetland destruction by creating or restoring a comparable number of wetland acres.

Section 404 has at least partially achieved its goal of preserving wetlands. Today, there are more than 110 million acres of wetlands in the United States, of which 95 percent are freshwater and 5 percent are in marine or saltwater systems.[5] Although the goal of "no net loss" of wetland acreage has not been met, section 404 has slowed the rate of destruction of wetlands from 290,000 acres annually between the mid-1970s and mid-1980s to 13,800 acres annually from 2004 to 2009.[6] The U.S. Fish & Wildlife Service will report on wetland losses from 2009 through 2019 in a report due for publication in 2022.[7] Current wetland losses may be attributed to urban development, agriculture, mining, and rural development.

---

4. United States v. Riverside Bayview Homes, Inc., 474 U.S. 121, 132 (1985) (discussing H.R. Rep. No. 92-911, at 76 (1972) (specifying that the "integrity" of waters intended to be protected by the CWA extends to the "condition in which the natural structure and function of ecosystems [are] maintained")).

5. *See* U.S. Fish & Wildlife Serv., Status and Trends of Wetlands in the Conterminous United States 2004 to 2009, at 16 (Sept. 2011), http://www.fws.gov/wetlands/Documents/Status-and-Trends-of-Wetlands-in-the-Conterminous-United-States-2004-to-2009.pdf.

6. *See id.* at 40.

7. *See* U.S. Fish & Wildlife Serv., Wetlands Status and Trends Reports, at 1 (Jan. 2020), https://www.fws.gov/wetlands/documents/Wetlands-Status-and-Trends-Reports-Fact-Sheet.pdf.

8.2 Jurisdictional Issues

The U.S. Army Corps of Engineers and the U.S. Environmental Protection Agency (EPA) jointly implement section 404, with the Corps primarily responsible for administering the permit program, and EPA retaining the right to veto or limit proposed permits and to prohibit use of locations in advance of a permit application. The Corps's permitting authority extends to the discharge of dredged or fill material in interstate waters, navigable waters affecting interstate commerce, waters subject to the ebb and flow of the tide, and other aquatic environments affecting regulated waters, such as adjacent wetlands.[8]

Since the enactment of section 404 as part of the 1972 amendments, Congress has expanded the Corps's jurisdiction in some respects while contracting it in others. To illustrate, in the early years of the section 404 permit program, the Corps understood its mandate broadly to include regulation of wetlands, an interpretation to which Congress acquiesced.[9] However, by 1977, Congress limited the mandate by exempting under section 404(f) routine agricultural and mining activity from the permitting process,[10] and by authorizing the Corps to issue general national or regional permits for categories of activity that it determines will have minimal adverse effects as specified in section 404(e).[11] All other discharges fall under the Corps's individual permit authority and are subject to an intensive review process.

In contrast to the National Pollutant Discharge Elimination System (NPDES) program, the section 404 permitting process involves a high degree of discretion rather than fixed, scientific standards. By requiring the Corps to balance environmental and socioeconomic factors when reviewing a permit,[12] the process aims to find ways to allow development while minimizing harm to the environment. Section 404 is similar to an NPDES scheme in that it presumes the existence of a less harmful way of pursuing development and places the burden on the applicant to show that this cannot be achieved.[13]

---

8. *See* 33 C.F.R. § 328.3(a).
9. *Riverside Bayview Homes*, 474 U.S. at 136–37.
10. *See* 33 U.S.C. § 1344(f).
11. *See id.* § 1344(e).
12. *See* 33 C.F.R. § 320.4.
13. *See* 40 C.F.R. § 230.10.

As is the case with respect to NPDES permits, a state can apply to EPA to take over issuance of section 404 permits within its boundaries.[14] To date, only three states—Michigan, New Jersey, and Florida—have obtained such authority,[15] and EPA nevertheless retains authority to review proposed permits and to transfer permitting authority to the Corps if it is not satisfied with the state's proposed permit.[16]

8.3 Definitional Issues and Scope

The scope of section 404 is based on current judicial and administrative interpretations of the core terms of the statute.

8.3.1 "Discharge" of "Dredged Material" and "Fill Material" Defined

The statutory definition of "discharge" is incorporated into the definitions of "discharge of dredged material" and "discharge of fill material" in 33 C.F.R. § 323.2(d) and 323.2(f), respectively. As discussed in Chapter 3, the Clean Water Act defines discharge as "any addition of any pollutant to navigable waters from any point source."[17] Redeposits of materials can constitute an "addition of a pollutant" under the CWA.

Dredged material is defined as any material dredged or excavated from the waters of the United States,[18] while fill material is "material placed in waters of the United States where the material

14. The standards for such application are at 40 C.F.R. pt. 233.

15. *State and Tribal Assumption of Section 404 of the Clean Water Act, U.S. Interactive Map of State and Tribal Assumption under CWA Section 404*, EPA, https://www.epa.gov/cwa404g/us-interactive-map-state-and-tribal-assumption-under-cwa-section-404 (last visited June 9, 2021); *State and Tribal Assumption of Section 404 of the Clean Water Act*, EPA, https://www.epa.gov/cwa404g (last visited June 9, 2021). As opposed to NPDES permitting authority, which almost all states have, that only three states have obtained section 404 authority has been viewed as a reflection of how difficult, complicated, and controversial the section 404 programs are. Other states that started down the road of seeking section 404 permitting authority were dissuaded by the complications that Michigan and New Jersey (the first two authorized states) were experiencing. *See generally* Ronald K. Gaddie & James L. Regens, Regulating Wetlands Protection: Environmental Federalism and the States (SUNY Press 1999).

16. 40 C.F.R. § 233.50.

17. CWA § 502(12), 33 U.S.C. § 1362(12).

18. *See* 33 C.F.R. § 323.2(c).

has the effect of: (i) Replacing any portion of a water of the United States with dry land; or (ii) [c]hanging the bottom elevation of any portion of a water of the United States."[19] The definition of fill material excludes trash or garbage, but includes such things as rock, sand, soil, clay, plastics, construction debris, wood chips, overburden from mining or other excavation activities, and materials used to create any structure or infrastructure in the waters of the United States.[20] "Discharge of fill material" is defined as "the addition of fill material into waters of the United States" and includes activities such as placement of fill material to facilitate construction in a water of the United States.[21] A "discharge of dredged material" includes "any addition of dredged material into, including redeposit of dredged material other than incidental fallback within, the waters of the United States."[22]

The concept of "fallback"—the incidental deposition of dredged material into a regulated water—has been controversial. Examples include soil that falls back into a wetland as it is being cleared of trees or material dredged from a riverbed that falls back into the river water. The controversial "Tulloch" rule, which required a permit for *any* discharge of such fallback material, was overturned in 1998 in *National Mining Association v. U.S. Army Corps of Engineers*[23] but has since been reinstated in a revised form.[24]

The definition of "fill material" was critical to the Fourth Circuit's holding in *Kentuckians for the Commonwealth, Inc. v. Rivenburgh*, in which environmental groups challenged the Corps's issuance of a section 404 permit to a mountaintop mining operator to fill large valley areas with excess mining spoil and thereby bury large areas of streams.[25] Plaintiffs argued that the mining spoil was not "fill" but waste and, as such, required an NPDES permit, not a section 404 permit. The district court had held that a section 404 permit can authorize discharge into waters only for some beneficial primary purpose, and cannot authorize waste material discharged solely to dispose of waste. The Fourth

19. 67 Fed. Reg. 31,129, 31,142 (May 9, 2002).
20. *See id.*
21. 33 C.F.R. § 323.2(f).
22. *Id.* § 323.2(d).
23. *See* 145 F.3d 1399 (D.C. Cir. 1998).
24. *See* 33 C.F.R. § 323.2(d)(3).
25. 317 F.3d 425 (4th Cir. 2003).

Circuit panel disagreed, finding the Corps's interpretation of "fill material" in section 404 "to mean all material that displaces water or changes the bottom elevation of a water body except for 'waste'—meaning garbage, sewage, and effluent that could be regulated by ongoing effluent limitations" under section 402.[26]

In *Coeur Alaska, Inc. v. Southeast Alaska Conservation Council*, an environmental group challenged a section 404 permit to discharge gold mine tailings into a lake.[27] As in *Rivenburgh*, plaintiffs argued that the mining company should have applied for a section 402 permit rather than a 404 permit, and that the discharges would violate new source performance standards under section 306. The Supreme Court disagreed, finding that "if the Corps has authority to issue a permit for a discharge under [section] 404, then the EPA lacks authority to do so under [section] 402."[28] The Court further noted: "Even if there were ambiguity on this point, the EPA's own regulations would resolve it. Those regulations provide that '[d]ischarges of dredged or fill material into waters of the United States which are regulated under section 404 of CWA' . . . 'do not require [section 402] permits' from the EPA."[29] The Court also declined to conclude that the section 306 performance standards would apply to the discharge.

8.3.2 "Navigable Waters" and "Waters of the United States" Defined

The definition of "navigable waters" is set forth in 33 U.S.C. § 1362, which refers to "waters of the United States, including the territorial seas."[30] As discussed at length in Chapter 3, the scope of federal jurisdiction and definition of "waters of the United States" has been the subject of multiple Supreme Court decisions, several EPA and Corps rulemakings, and a tremendous amount of litigation, and remains perhaps the most significant and unresolved issue under the Clean Water Act.

---

26. *Id.* at 448.
27. *See* 557 U.S. 261 (2009).
28. *Id.* at 274.
29. *Id.*
30. CWA § 502(7), 33 U.S.C. § 1362(7).

8.3.3 "Wetlands" Defined

Both EPA and the Corps define wetlands as "areas that are inundated or saturated by surface or ground water at a frequency and duration sufficient to support, and that under normal circumstances do support, a prevalence of vegetation typically adapted for life in saturated soil conditions. Wetlands generally include swamps, marshes, bogs, and similar areas."[31] In 1985, the Supreme Court in *United States v. Riverside Bayview Homes, Inc.* established Corps jurisdiction over certain wetland areas, finding the Corps's regulation of wetlands that are "inseparably bound up" with the aquatic ecosystems of navigable waters to be consistent with congressional intent in the Clean Water Act.[32] As discussed more generally in Chapter 3, in order to fall under CWA jurisdiction, an area must both qualify as "wetlands" and meet the regulatory criteria for "waters of the United States."

To determine whether an area is "wetlands," as opposed to uplands, in the first place, the Corps typically uses the criteria set forth in the 1987 Corps of Engineers Wetlands Delineation Manual and the Corps guidance interpreting the Manual to determine the existence of wetlands. Courts generally afford significant deference to the Corps's determination of whether an area is a wetland.

8.3.4 Review of Jurisdictional Determinations

Recently, in 2016, in *U.S. Army Corps of Engineers v. Hawkes Co.*, the Supreme Court reversed Circuit Court precedent and held that jurisdictional determinations by the Corps may be challenged judicially as a final agency action.[33] The *Hawkes* decision followed on the heels of an earlier opinion, from 2012, *Sackett v. EPA*,[34] in which the Supreme Court held that there is an immediate right to judicial review of an EPA administrative order issued in a wetlands case.

Despite using identical definitions for wetlands and "waters of the United States," the Corps and EPA may come to different conclusions about whether a given area is subject to section 404 based on different scientific methodologies. In 1979, the U.S.

31. 40 C.F.R. § 230.41(a)(1); 33 C.F.R. § 328.3(c).
32. 474 U.S. 121, 134 (1985).
33. 136 S. Ct. 1807 (2016).
34. 566 U.S. 120 (2012).

Attorney General opined that EPA has ultimate authority over determining the scope of waters of the United States for purposes of section 404.[35] Therefore, even if the Corps determines it does not have authority to require a permit for a given discharge because it does not have jurisdiction over the area, EPA may override that decision.

8.4 Section 404 Permitting Process

8.4.1 Exemptions

As specified in section 404(f), several broad categories of activity are exempt from the permitting process, including discharges of dredged and fill material resulting from the following: normal farming, silvicultural, and ranching activities; maintenance of dams and bridges; construction of certain irrigation or sedimentation systems; construction of forest and farm roads; and some state-approved projects.[36] In general, routine discharges in the course of ongoing activity are exempt, while one-time discharges resulting in permanent alterations are not. For instance, in *United States v. Brace*,[37] a Third Circuit panel held that the conversion of wetlands in order to make the area suitable for farming was not "normal" farm activity and therefore not covered by the exemption.

The "recapture" provision of the Clean Water Act, section 404(f)(2), excludes from the section 404(f) exemption "[a]ny discharge of dredged or fill material into the navigable waters incidental to any activity having as its purpose bringing an area of the navigable waters into a use to which it was not previously subject, where the flow or circulation of navigable waters may be impaired or the reach of such waters be reduced."[38] Thus, normal plowing can be regulated if it falls within the recapture provision.

---

35. *See* Memorandum of Agreement between the Department of the Army and the Environmental Protection Agency Concerning the Determination of the Section 404 Program and the Application of the Exemptions under Section 404(f) of the Clean Water Act (Jan. 19, 1989), http://water.epa.gov/lawsregs/guidance/wetlands/404f.cfm.

36. *See* CWA § 404(f), 33 U.S.C. § 1344(f).

37. *See* 41 F.3d 117 (3d Cir. 1994).

38. *See* CWA § 404(f)(2), 33 U.S.C. § 1344(f)(2).

Converting ranch land to orchards by deep ripping falls within the recapture provision, where destruction of the soil layer constitutes an impairment of the flow of nearby navigable waters.[39] The Corps has issued detailed regulations for determining whether an activity is exempt.[40]

8.4.2 Individual Permitting: Overview

An individual permit usually is required for potentially significant impacts, as opposed to a general permit, which is required for discharges with minimal adverse effects. Pursuant to section 404(b)(1) and implementing regulations, the Corps conducts a public interest review when considering whether to permit a discharge that would damage wetlands. The Corps first determines the impact a given discharge would have on the public interest by looking at a spectrum of factors such as economics, aesthetics, and flood control.[41] The Corps then weighs any benefits that "reasonably may be expected" to accrue as a result of pursuing alternatives to the proposed discharge against "foreseeable detriments" caused by the proposed discharge.[42] In balancing these considerations, the Corps ultimately must base its determination on the environmental effects of a proposed project and its alternatives, and it may not deny a permit based on socioeconomic factors alone.[43] In November 2020, the Corps made national news headlines when it denied a permit for the controversial Pebble Mine project in Alaska. The project sought to create the biggest gold, copper, and molybdenum mine in North America, but the Corps found it "does not comply with Clean Water Act guidelines" and "is contrary to the public interest."[44] In early 2021, the project developer appealed the permit denial and the Corps

---

39. *See* Borden Ranch P'ship v. U.S. Army Corps of Eng'rs, 261 F.3d 810, 815 (9th Cir. 2001), *aff'd per curiam*, 537 U.S. 99 (2002).

40. *See* 33 C.F.R. § 323.4.

41. *See id.* § 320.4.

42. *See id.*

43. The procedural requirements for public review hearings are contained in 33 C.F.R. part 327.

44. Bill Weir, *Army Corps Denies Permit for Controversial Mine That Threatened Salmon Habitat in Alaska*, CNN (Nov. 25, 2020, 6:36 PM), https://www.cnn.com/2020/11/25/politics/pebble-mine-alaska-permit-denied/index.html.

agreed to reconsider its decision, noting its reconsideration process could take more than a year.[45]

In 1980, EPA issued guidelines for the actual decision-making process contained in section 404(b)(1) to ensure that effects on ecosystems remained the primary factor considered by the Corps in issuing permits. Compliance with these guidelines is a requirement governing the Corps's public interest review.[46] According to the guidelines,[47] a permit will issue if (1) no practicable alternative exists; (2) no significant adverse impacts on aquatic resources will result; (3) all reasonable mitigation measures are employed; and (4) the proposed project does not violate other statutes. These guidelines also indicate the factors that EPA will use in its administrative review of a permit decision. Section 404(c) authorizes EPA to veto or restrict an individual permit after notice and opportunity for public hearing if the discharge would have an unacceptable adverse impact on municipal water supplies, shellfish and fishing areas, wildlife, or recreational uses.[48] Section 404(c) also authorizes EPA to bar use of areas for discharges even absent a pending permit application.

In *Mingo Logan Coal Co. v. U.S. EPA*, the D.C. Circuit endorsed a broad veto power for EPA under section 404(c), finding that the statute grants EPA "authority to prohibit/deny/restrict/withdraw a specification at any time," including after permit issuance by the Corps.[49] The Corps had issued a section 404 permit to Mingo Logan Coal Company in 2007 for a mountaintop coal mining operation in West Virginia, authorizing the discharge of dredged or fill material from the mine into three streams and their tributaries. EPA did not exercise its veto authority until four years later, in 2011, when it withdrew the permit's discharge specifications. In 2013, the D.C. Circuit found that EPA's retroactive withdrawal was permissible because the statute "imposes no temporal limit," and in 2016, the D.C. Circuit upheld EPA's withdrawal as neither arbitrary nor capricious.[50]

45. Becky Bohrer, *Appeal Review for Pebble Mine Could Take Over a Year, Army Corps of Engineers Says*, ANCHORAGE DAILY NEWS (May 27, 2021), https://www.adn.com/business-economy/2021/05/27/appeal-review-for-pebble-mine-could-take-over-a-year-says-army-corps-of-engineers/.

46. *See* 33 C.F.R. § 320.4.

47. *See* 40 C.F.R. § 230.10(a)–(d).

48. *See* 33 U.S.C. § 1344(c).

49. *See* 714 F.3d 608, 613 (D.C. Cir. 2013).

50. *Id.*; Mingo Logan Coal Co. v. EPA, 829 F.3d 710 (D.C. Cir. 2016).

8.4.2.1 Defining Project Purpose

An applicant for an individual permit must first define the purpose of a proposed project. If the Corps agrees that the project is "water dependent,"[51] the applicant bears a lesser burden in terms of showing the existence of practicable alternatives.[52] Even if a project is not water dependent, whether the purpose of the project is defined to require features unique to the proposed site can influence how far an applicant must look for practicable alternatives. For instance, a permit applicant proposing an amusement park on a given site will have to consider any practicable alternative meeting its broadly defined project needs. When a project purpose is defined by more particularized market and geographical details, the universe of practicable alternatives shrinks to only those sites meeting whatever specifications the Corps determines are necessary to fulfill the project's purpose. According to the public interest review factors, the Corps must give some deference to the applicant's purpose as influenced by economic and logistical feasibility.[53]

8.4.2.2 Practicable Alternatives Test

If a proposed project is not water dependent, an applicant for an individual permit must overcome two presumptions. First, the Corps will presume the existence of a "practicable alternative" to the proposed discharge.[54] Moreover, an alternative is practicable when it is possible for the applicant to fulfill the "overall purpose" of the project at the alternative site or using alternative methods taking into account "cost, existing technology, and logistics."[55] This provision also specifies that an alternative site that is not owned by the applicant will be considered a practicable

51. "Where the activity associated with a discharge which is proposed for a special aquatic site does not require access or proximity to or siting within the special aquatic site in question to fulfill its basic purpose (i.e., is not 'water dependent'), practicable alternatives that do not involve special aquatic sites are presumed to be available, unless clearly demonstrated otherwise. In addition, where a discharge is proposed for a special aquatic site, all practicable alternatives to the proposed discharge which do not involve a discharge into a special aquatic site are presumed to have less adverse impact on the aquatic ecosystem, unless clearly demonstrated otherwise." 40 C.F.R. § 230.10(a)(3).

52. *See* 40 C.F.R. § 230.10(a)(3).

53. *See, e.g.*, Sylvester v. U.S. Army Corps of Eng'rs, 882 F.2d 407 (9th Cir. 1989) ("[A]n alternative site does not have to accommodate components of a project that are merely incidental to the applicant's basic purpose.").

54. 40 C.F.R. § 230.10(a)(3).

55. *Id.* § 230.10(a)(2).

alternative if it is within the applicant's ability to acquire the site. Second, the Corps will presume that any practicable alternative that does not involve a discharge will have a lesser impact on the aquatic ecosystem than the proposed discharge.[56] EPA has determined that the bounds of the universe of practicable alternatives are determined by looking at the time when the applicant entered the market to acquire the site of the proposed project, not at the time of permit application.[57]

8.4.2.3 Mitigation

Prior to April 2008, guidance regarding compensatory mitigation requirements for permitted impacts to wetlands existed in a patchwork of national documents issued by the Corps and EPA at various points over the course of 17 years (often in conjunction with other agencies such as the U.S. Fish and Wildlife Service).[58] In response to concerns about the "consistent, predictable and equitable interpretation and application of these guidance documents," EPA and the Corps issued revised regulations for compensatory mitigation.[59]

Consistent with the provisions of section 404(b)(1), the regulations require applicants to take all appropriate and practicable measures to minimize adverse impacts to waters and to rely on compensatory mitigation only for unavoidable impacts.[60] The regulations further require that when considering mitigation matters, the Corps must identify environmentally preferable options by evaluating the likelihood of ecological success and sustainability, comparing the location and significance of the mitigation site to the impact on the watershed and costs of the project.[61] The regulations express a preference for mitigation measures in the same watershed as the impacts, as well as for restoration (or "[r]e-establishment or rehabilitation . . . with the goal of returning natural or historic functions and characteristics to a former or

56. *See id.* § 230.10(a)(3).
57. *See* Bersani v. U.S. EPA, 850 F.2d 36 (2d Cir. 1988) (clarifying and validating EPA's "market entry theory" of when practicable alternatives available to an applicant are to be evaluated).
58. 73 Fed. Reg. 19,594, 19,595 (Apr. 10, 2008).
59. *Id.*
60. *See* 33 C.F.R. § 332.1(c).
61. *See* 73 Fed. Reg. at 19,627.

degraded wetland") versus other methods of mitigation.[62] The regulations also "retain[] a preference for in-kind mitigation," that is, of a similar type to the affected resource.[63] Finally, the regulations establish a hierarchy for implementation of mitigation options, with the "most preferred" option being wetland mitigation bank credits and the least preferred being "[p]ermittee-responsible mitigation through off-site and/or out-of-kind mitigation."[64]

Under the regulations, wetland mitigation banks have flourished, with thousands of bank sites now created across the United States. A wetland mitigation bank is a physical wetland area that has been restored, established, enhanced, or preserved as a form of compensation for permitted wetland impacts; section 404 permit holders purchase "compensatory mitigation credits" from a bank owner. The credits represent physical wetland area maintained at the bank site.[65]

In 2015, EPA and the Corps released a report summarizing the progress made in implementing the 2008 mitigation regulations.[66] The report found that under the regulations, only approximately 10 percent of permit authorizations by the Corps required compensatory mitigation, because of the stringent requirements to avoid and minimize adverse impacts.[67]

In June 2018, EPA and the Corps signed a Memorandum of Agreement to provide greater flexibilities for compensatory mitigation in Alaska, "given the abundance of wetlands and unique circumstances involved with Section 404 permitting in the state."[68] The Memorandum of Agreement recognized several "guiding principles that are specific to the state of Alaska," including allowing out-of-kind compensatory mitigation, mitigation over a larger watershed scale and on public land, and "a less

---

62. EPA, *Wetlands Compensatory Mitigation*, https://nepis.epa.gov/Exe/ZyPURL.cgi?Dockey=P1003CO2.TXT (last visited July 14, 2022).

63. *See* 73 Fed. Reg. at 19,632.

64. 33 C.F.R. § 332.3(b).

65. *Mitigation Banks under CWA Section 404*, EPA, https://www.epa.gov/cwa-404/mitigation-banks-under-cwa-section-404 (last updated Mar. 24, 2021).

66. Inst. for Water Res., 2015-R-03, The Mitigation Rule Retrospective: A Review of the 2008 Regulations Governing Compensatory Mitigation for Losses of Aquatic Resources (Oct. 2015), https://www.epa.gov/cwa-404/mitigation-rule-retrospective-review-2008-regulations-governing-compensatory-mitigation.

67. *See id.* at 11.

68. *Compensatory Mitigation in Alaska under CWA Section 404*, EPA, https://www.epa.gov/cwa-404/compensatory-mitigation-alaska-under-cwa-section-404 (last updated June 2, 2021).

rigorous permit review for small projects with minor environmental impacts."[69]

8.4.3 Issuance of General Permits

A general permit is required for a discharge with minimal adverse effects. Section 404(e) authorizes the Corps to issue general permits for certain activities on a regional, statewide, or nationwide basis. After a public notice and comment period, the Corps may issue a general permit only upon finding that the activities in a category (1) are similar in nature, (2) will cause only minimal adverse environmental effects when performed separately, and (3) will have only minimal cumulative adverse effects on the environment.[70] The Corps further specifies that duplication of regulation by another federal, state, or local agency also will influence whether a general permit is issued.[71] These general permits may be effective for up to five years and are revocable by the Corps if a review and public comment period reveals that the activity is having a negative impact on the environment or if the activity is more appropriately authorized by an individual permit.[72]

8.4.4 Nationwide Permits

The most important category of general permits is the nationwide permit (NWP) program, administered pursuant to 33 C.F.R. part 330. This program is expressly designed to "regulate with little, if any, delay or paperwork certain activities having minimal impact."[73] There currently are over 50 NWP categories that authorize approximately 35,000 reported activities, including residential developments, utility lines, road crossings, mining activities, and commercial shellfish aquaculture activities.[74] Even if an activity falls within a specified NWP category, the Corps is authorized to require issuance of an individual permit under section

---

69. *See id.*
70. CWA § 404(e)(1), 33 U.S.C. § 1344(e)(1).
71. *See Obtain a Permit*, U.S. Army Corps of Eng'rs, https://www.usace.army.mil/Missions/Civil-Works/Regulatory-Program-and-Permits/Obtain-a-Permit/ (last visited June 14, 2021).
72. CWA § 404(e)(2), 33 U.S.C. § 1344(e)(2).
73. 33 C.F.R. § 330.1(b).
74. *See* U.S. Army Corps of Eng'rs, Fact Sheet: Nationwide Permit Reissuance (Jan. 2021), https://usace.contentdm.oclc.org/utils/getfile/collection/p16021coll7/id/16919.

404(b)(1) if it finds that the environmental impact is more than minimal.[75]

After the reissuance of nationwide permits in 2017, there was significant litigation and regulatory activity surrounding NWP 12, which has been used to authorize activities associated with the construction, maintenance, and repair of utility line crossings, including oil and natural gas pipelines. In 2020, in litigation over the controversial Keystone XL pipeline, the Montana federal district court issued a nationwide injunction vacating the use of NWP 12 for the construction of new oil and gas pipelines, and the Ninth Circuit denied the Corps's emergency request to lift the injunction pending the Corps's appeal. The Supreme Court then overturned the nationwide injunction and limited the district court's decision to the construction of the Keystone XL pipeline.[76] In January 2021, the Corps reissued NWP 12, splitting it into three new nationwide permits, for the construction of oil and gas pipelines, electric and telecommunications lines, and water and sewer lines, respectively.[77]

8.5 Noncompliance and Enforcement

Enforcement of section 404 is, in most respects, similar to other CWA enforcement, which is discussed in Chapter 12. In 1989, EPA and the Corps—both of which have broad enforcement authority—issued a memorandum of agreement allocating enforcement responsibility, with most activity undertaken by the Corps. The memorandum provides that the Corps will take lead responsibility for all enforcement matters involving violations of section 404 permits, as well as for most enforcement matters involving allegations of unpermitted discharges, except those meeting specified criteria for which EPA would take the lead.[78] EPA-led matters are those involving repeat violators, flagrant violations, specific

75. 33 C.F.R. § 330.1(c).

76. *See* U.S. Army Corps of Eng'rs v. N. Plains Res. Council, 141 S. Ct. 190 (2020).

77. *See* 86 Fed. Reg. 2744 (Jan. 13, 2021).

78. Memorandum between the Department of the Army and the Environmental Protection Agency (Jan. 1989), https://www.epa.gov/cwa-404/federal-enforcement-section-404-program-clean-water-act.

requests by EPA, or cases in which the Corps recommends that EPA bring an administrative penalty action.[79]

8.6 Challenges to Corps Determinations

8.6.1 Fifth Amendment Takings Issues

Particularly in the context of wetlands regulation, one frequent challenge to Corps section 404 permitting decisions is that denial of a permit amounts to a taking of property by the government without "just compensation," which is prohibited by the Fifth Amendment of the U.S. Constitution.[80] In *United States v. Riverside Bayview Homes*, a case involving the denial of a section 404 permit, the Supreme Court held that "the mere assertion of regulatory jurisdiction by a governmental body does not constitute a regulatory taking."[81] The Court went on to specify, however, that when denial of a permit resulted in the prevention of all economically viable uses for the land, such regulation would constitute a taking. This was echoed in another opinion regarding the state regulation of wetlands, *Lucas v. South Carolina Coastal Council*,[82] in which the Supreme Court held that a regulation denying a landowner all economically viable use of his property creates a presumption of an unlawful taking.

In *Palazzolo v. Rhode Island*,[83] the Supreme Court addressed the issue of whether a landowner was entitled to compensation when it was denied a permit to fill protected coastal wetlands. The Court rejected the state's argument that there was no taking because the regulation protecting the wetlands predated the owner's obtaining title. The Court did acknowledge that land-use restrictions that were part of the background principles of state law would not give rise to takings. The Court agreed with the state that all economical use of the property had not been deprived because the uplands portions of the property could still be improved, and remanded for consideration of whether a taking claim could nonetheless be established.

79. *Id.*

80. U.S. Const. amend. V (prohibiting the federal government from taking "private property" for public use without just compensation).

81. 474 U.S. 121, 126 (1985).

82. 505 U.S. 1003 (1992).

83. 533 U.S. 606 (2001).

More recently, in *Koontz v. St. Johns River Water Management District*,[84] the Supreme Court addressed a taking challenge in the context of Florida wetlands law. The petitioner was denied a permit to build on a wetland by the District because the petitioner was not willing to deed a large conservation easement to the District or hire contractors to make improvements to District-owned wetlands several miles away. The Court ruled that the District's demands for property and money must each have a nexus and rough proportionality to the effects of the proposed land use, even though the District denied the permit and no property was actually taken.

8.6.2 Commerce Clause Challenges

Expansive regulation of wetlands by the Corps has also been challenged on the grounds that this regulation exceeds the power granted Congress under the Commerce Clause of the U.S. Constitution.[85] The commerce power of Congress had long been thought to be virtually all-encompassing, but recent Supreme Court decisions have reaffirmed historical limitations on the commerce power.[86] Courts have concluded that Congress intended the scope of the Clean Water Act to be only as broad as that permitted under the Commerce Clause.[87] Some parties have argued, however, that the regulatory manifestation of that scope, as promulgated and implemented by the Corps, in fact exceeds the commerce power. Up to now, the Supreme Court and lower courts considering this argument have avoided deciding this constitutional question by instead concluding that the Corps regulations exceed the authority granted by Congress. Thus, in *SWANCC*, as discussed in Chapter 3, the Court interpreted the CWA as precluding the expanded regulatory jurisdiction the Corps was seeking to assert. It did not address the issue of whether, if the CWA were interpreted to allow for such expansive jurisdiction, it would be constitutional.[88]

---

84. 570 U.S. 595 (2013).

85. U.S. Const. art. I, § 8, cl. 3.

86. *See* Nat'l Fed'n of Indep. Bus. v. Sebelius, 567 U.S. 519 (2012); United States v. Morrison, 529 U.S. 598 (2000); United States v. Lopez, 514 U.S. 549 (1995).

87. *See, e.g.*, Rueth v. U.S. EPA, 13 F.3d 227, 231 (7th Cir. 1993).

88. Solid Waste Agency of N. Cook Cnty. v. U.S. Army Corps of Eng'rs, 531 U.S. 159 (2001); *see* United States v. Wilson, 133 F.3d 251 (4th Cir. 1997).

9 Discharges and Spills of Oil and Hazardous Substances

9.1 Introduction

In recognition of the potentially catastrophic effects on the environment and public health of a spill of oil or hazardous substances, the Clean Water Act (CWA) provides for special regulation of these discharges.[1] Specifically, section 311 of the CWA declares as the "policy of the United States that there should be no discharge of oil or hazardous substances into or upon the navigable waters of the United States, adjoining shorelines," or other enumerated locations. Section 311 also imposes higher standards of care in the management and movement of oil, including the requirement of spill prevention plans; it enables the government to recover the costs of cleaning up oil and hazardous substance discharges; and it provides for the imposition of penalties for such discharges. Moreover, following the 1989 *Exxon Valdez* spill in Alaska, Congress enacted the Oil Pollution Act (OPA),[2] amending section 311 and establishing a comprehensive scheme for the cleanup of oil spills, including a mechanism to impose liability for such spills. This chapter addresses the statutory and regulatory

---

1. *See* CWA § 311, 33 U.S.C. § 1321.
2. *See* OPA, 33 U.S.C. §§ 2701–2761.

provisions regarding spills and discharges of oil and hazardous substances and includes a discussion of OPA.

9.2 Section 311(b)(3): The Prohibition of Discharges

Section 311(b)(3) prohibits the discharge of oil or hazardous substances in such quantities as may be harmful, unless certain exceptions apply. The discharge must be

> into or upon the navigable waters of the United States, adjoining shorelines, or into or upon the waters of the contiguous zone, or . . . in connection with activities under the Outer Continental Shelf Lands Act[3] or the Deepwater Port Act of 1974,[4] or which may affect natural resources belonging to, appertaining to, or under the exclusive management authority of the United States (including resources under the Magnuson-Stevens Fishery Conservation and Management Act).[5]

The regulatory definitions of "navigable waters" for purposes of section 311 are very similar to the definitions of "waters of the United States" for purposes of the section 301 prohibition of discharges. In other words, "navigable waters" includes all manner of waters and wetlands with interstate commerce connections.[6] "Contiguous zone" is defined to include the territorial sea and the larger 200-mile contiguous zone established by international treaty.[7] Significantly, "adjoining shoreline" is not defined in the statute or regulations. The U.S. Environmental Protection Agency (EPA) has asserted in enforcement cases that the term is not limited to close-to-water beach-type areas but includes all areas from

3. 43 U.S.C. §§ 1331–1356b.
4. 33 U.S.C. §§ 1501–1524.
5. *See* CWA § 311(b)(3), 33 U.S.C. § 1321(b)(3).
6. *Compare* 40 C.F.R. § 110.1 (definition of "navigable waters" for the purposes of oil discharges), *and* 40 C.F.R. § 116.3 (definition of "navigable waters" for the purposes of hazardous substance discharges), *with* 40 C.F.R. § 122.2 (definition of "waters of the United States" for purpose of NPDES program).
7. *See* CWA § 311(a)(9), 33 U.S.C. § 1321(a)(9). "Contiguous zone" means the entire zone established or to be established by the United States under article 24 of the Convention on the Territorial Sea and the Contiguous Zone. *See* CWA § 311(a)(9), 33 U.S.C. § 1321(a)(9).

which discharged oil or hazardous substances can migrate to waters.[8]

9.2.1 "Oil" and "Hazardous Substance" Defined

Both "oil" and "hazardous substance" are defined terms. "Oil" is defined by the statute as "oil of any kind or in any form, including, but not limited to, petroleum, fuel oil, sludge, oil refuse, and oil mixed with wastes other than dredged spoil."[9] Since "oil" is not limited to "petroleum," it includes animal and vegetable oils as well.[10] "Hazardous substance" is defined by EPA in the form of a list of almost 300 elements and compounds, and includes any isomers and hydrates as well as solutions and mixtures containing these substances.[11]

9.2.2 "Discharge" Defined

The term "discharge" also is defined broadly for section 311 purposes. It "includes, but is not limited to, any spilling, leaking, pumping, pouring, emitting, emptying or dumping."[12] Unlike section 301, section 311's prohibition of discharges is not premised on the discharges emanating from a point source. There are exclusions to the definition of discharge for purposes of the section 311 prohibition, the most important being the exclusion of a discharge that is in compliance with a National Pollutant Discharge Elimination System (NPDES) permit under section 402. A discharge is "in compliance with a permit under Section 402 of the Act" if the permit contains an effluent limitation specifically applicable to the substance discharged (or an effluent limitation applicable to another waste parameter that has been specifically identified in the permit as intended to limit such substance).[13] Other exclusions include discharges resulting from circumstances that were identified, reviewed, and made a part of the public record with respect to the NPDES permit and subject

8. *See* United States v. Colonial Pipeline Co., 242 F. Supp. 2d 1365 (N.D. Ga. 2002).

9. CWA § 311(a)(1), 33 U.S.C. § 1321(a)(1). "Sludge" is defined as an aggregate of oil or oil and other matter of any kind in any form other than dredged spoil having a combined specific gravity equivalent to or greater than water. *See* 40 C.F.R. § 110.1.

10. *See* 40 C.F.R. § 112.2 (definition of "non-petroleum oil").

11. *See id.* § 116.4.

12. CWA § 311(a)(2), 33 U.S.C. § 1321(a)(2).

13. 40 C.F.R. § 117.12(b).

to a permit condition[14] and "continuous or anticipated intermittent discharges," which are identified in a facility's NPDES permit or permit application and which are caused by events occurring within the scope of a facility's operating or treatment systems.[15]

9.2.3 "Quantities as May Be Harmful" Defined

Section 311 prohibits only those discharges in "quantities as may be harmful." Congress tasked the President with defining this by regulations, but noting in the statutory text that the phrase includes harm to the public health or welfare or the environment of the United States, including but not limited to fish, shellfish, wildlife, and public and private property, shorelines, and beaches.[16] The regulations define the phrase "quantities as may be harmful" for both oil and hazardous substances.[17] For oil, it means quantities that either violate applicable water quality standards,[18] cause a film or a sheen upon or discoloration of the surface of the water or adjoining shorelines, or cause a sludge or emulsion to be deposited beneath the surface of the water or upon adjoining shorelines;[19] for "hazardous substances," EPA defines the term "quantities as may be harmful" as the reportable quantities set forth in the table at 40 C.F.R. § 117.3.[20] These levels range from one pound (for pesticides such as aldrin, DDT, dieldrin, and chlordane) up to 5,000 pounds (for substances such as hydrochloric acid and sodium phosphate). Discharges in excess of the prescribed levels are prohibited. There are ten enumerated exceptions to this definition, composed of discharges in compliance with one of the listed provisions or mechanisms, mostly under the federal environmental laws.[21] These include, for example, such things as certain discharges to a publicly owned treatment

14. This exclusion is defined at 40 C.F.R. § 117.12(c)(1)–(3).

15. CWA § 311(a)(2), 33 U.S.C. § 1321(a)(2); 40 C.F.R. § 116.3. This exclusion is defined at 40 C.F.R. § 117.12(d)(1)–(2).

16. CWA § 311(b)(4), 33 U.S.C. § 1321(b)(4).

17. 40 C.F.R. § 110.3.

18. "Applicable water quality standards" means state water quality standards adopted by the state pursuant to section 303 of the Clean Water Act or promulgated by EPA pursuant to that section. *See* 40 C.F.R. § 110.1.

19. *Id.* § 110.3. The addition of dispersants or emulsifiers to oil to be discharged so as to circumvent the provisions of this section is prohibited. *See id.* § 110.4.

20. 40 C.F.R. § 117.1(a) defines "reportable quantities" as quantities that may be harmful, the discharge of which is a violation of CWA section 311(b)(3).

21. 40 C.F.R. § 117.11.

works (POTW), discharges in conformity with a registered pesticide label, and discharges that comply with certain permits, such as a 404 permit under the Clean Water Act, permit conditions under the Resource Conservation and Recovery Act or the Marine Protection, Research, and Sanctuaries Act.[22]

9.3 Notice Requirements for Oil and Hazardous Substance Spills

Congress recognized that although oil and hazardous substances discharges can be prohibited, they cannot be totally prevented. Section 311, therefore, places great importance on immediate notification to the government when such discharges do occur. If a prohibited discharge occurs from a vessel[23] or an onshore[24] or offshore[25] facility, the person in charge of the vessel or facility is required to notify the appropriate federal agency as soon as he or she has knowledge of the prohibited discharge.[26] The federal agency, in turn, is to notify the appropriate state agencies. In the case of an oil spill, the person in charge is directed to notify the National Response Center (NRC). If reporting to the NRC is not practicable, reports may be made to the Coast Guard or EPA's predesignated on-scene coordinator for the geographic area where the discharge occurs. Reports must be made in accordance with procedures set forth in the Coast Guard regulations,[27] and in the

22. The full list of exclusions is at 40 C.F.R. § 117.11.

23. The term "vessel" is broadly defined as every description of watercraft or other artificial contrivance used, or capable of being used, as a means of transportation on water other than a public vessel. CWA § 311(a)(3), 33 U.S.C. § 1321(a)(3). A "public vessel" means a vessel owned or bareboat-chartered and operated by the United States, or by a state or political subdivision thereof, or by a foreign nation, except when such vessel is engaged in commerce. *See* CWA § 311(a)(4), 33 U.S.C. § 1321(a)(4).

24. An "onshore facility" means any facility (including but not limited to motor vehicles and rolling stock) of any kind located in, on, or under, any land within the United States other than submerged land. *See* CWA § 311(a)(10), 33 U.S.C. § 1321(a)(10).

25. An "offshore facility" means any facility of any kind located in, on, or under, any of the navigable waters of the United States, and any facility of any kind that is subject to the jurisdiction of the United States and is located in, on, or under any other waters, other than a vessel or a public vessel. *See* CWA § 311(a)(11), 33 U.S.C. § 1321(a)(11).

26. *See* CWA § 311(b)(5), 33 U.S.C. § 1321(b)(5); 40 C.F.R. § 110.6.

27. *See* 33 C.F.R. pt. 153, subpt. B.

National Oil and Hazardous Substances Pollution Contingency Plan.[28] This notification process helps ensure a fast and efficient response to stop the spill and mitigate its effects.

Similarly, the regulations require notification in the event of a significant spill of hazardous substances. Specifically, the person in charge of the vessel or facility involved is required to notify immediately the appropriate federal agency as soon as he or she has knowledge of any discharge of a designated hazardous substance from the vessel or facility in quantities that exceed the reportable quantity during a 24-hour period.[29] The notice must be given in accordance with the procedures set forth in Department of Transportation regulations.[30]

9.4 The Consequences of a Prohibited Discharge

Enforcement of section 311 is generally divided between the Coast Guard, which has primary responsibilities for vessels and marine transportation facilities, and EPA, which has responsibility for other facilities. The enforcement provisions of the CWA are discussed generally in Chapter 12. However, two unique provisions applicable to oil and hazardous substance discharges bear special mention.

9.4.1 Administrative and Civil Penalties

The CWA provides that the owner, operator, or person in charge of a vessel or facility from which a hazardous substance is discharged in violation of section 311(b)(3) is subject to a penalty, which can be sought administratively by either EPA or the Coast Guard, or judicially by the Department of Justice (DOJ).[31] In July 2021, the statutory limits (which have been adjusted by regulation for inflation) are the greater of $48,762 per day of violation or, in the case of oil, up to $1,951 per barrel discharged,

28. *See* 40 C.F.R. pt. 300, subpt. E.
29. *See id.* § 117.21.
30. *Id.* These regulations are promulgated at 33 C.F.R. § 153.203.
31. *See* CWA § 311(b)(6)(A), 33 U.S.C. § 1321(b)(6)(A). Administrative penalties are discussed at CWA § 311(b)(6)(B)–(I), 33 U.S.C. § 1321(b)(6)(B)–(I).

and in the case of hazardous substances, up to $1,951 per unit of reportable quantity discharged.[32] Since large oil or hazardous substance discharges may take place over a single day or a small number of days, the per-barrel-or-reportable-unit provision allows for large penalties for such events. If the spill resulted from gross negligence or willful misconduct, the maximum penalty is $5,783 (U.S. Army Corps of Engineers) or $5,851 (EPA) per barrel of oil or unit of reportable quantity of a hazardous substance.[33] EPA has taken the position that the maximum penalty is calculated on the total amount of the spill, not just the amount actually to reach water.[34]

The seminal case under OPA was the *Deepwater Horizon* oil spill. As of the time of publication, the *Deepwater Horizon* was the largest marine oil spill in history caused by the April 20, 2010, explosion on the *Deepwater Horizon* oil rig in the Gulf of Mexico, approximately 41 miles off the coast of Louisiana. One of the questions in the penalty calculation was whether penalties could be imposed on the 810,000 barrels of oil collected at the well head and placed in vessels. In the *Deepwater Horizon* litigation, the government agreed that penalties would not be imposed on the 810,000 barrels collected.[35]

In determining the total penalty, the court applies the appropriate dollar per barrel amount, multiplies by the number of barrels, and then moves up or down from this number applying the penalty factors:

> the . . . court . . . shall consider the seriousness of the violation or violations, the economic benefit to the violator, if any, resulting from the violation, the degree of culpability involved, any other penalty for the same incident, any history of prior violations, the nature, extent, and degree of success of any efforts of the violator to minimize or mitigate the effects of the discharge, the economic

32. *See* CWA § 311(b)(7)(A), 33 U.S.C. § 1321(b)(7)(A), with adjustments for inflation. EPA's inflation-adjusted penalties are set forth in 40 C.F.R. § 19.4.

33. *See* CWA § 311(b)(7)(D), 33 U.S.C. § 1321(b)(7)(D). *See* 40 C.F.R. § 19.4 (EPA inflation-adjusted penalties); 33 C.F.R. § 27.3 (Corps inflation-adjusted penalties).

34. *See* United States v. Colonial Pipeline Co., 242 F. Supp. 2d 1365, 1376–77 (N.D. Ga. 2002) (adopting EPA's position); *see also* United States v. CITGO Petroleum Corp., Civil Action No. 08-893 (W.D. La. Sept. 29, 2011).

35. *See In re* Oil Spill by the Oil Rig "Deepwater Horizon" in the Gulf of Mexico, on April 20, 2010, Findings of Fact and Conclusions of Law Phase Two Trial, 77 F. Supp. 3d 500, 522 ¶ 255 (E.D. La. 2015).

impact of the penalty on the violator, and any other matters as justice may require.[36]

The CWA does not define gross negligence or willful misconduct. The court in the *Deepwater Horizon* litigation held that federal law, not state tort law, governs the interpretation of these terms and that in evaluating the necessary standard of care, a greater risk means that a greater degree of care is required.[37]

9.4.2 Removal Authority

Section 311 directs the President (who has delegated this authority to the Coast Guard and EPA) to remove or arrange for the removal of a discharge, and mitigate or prevent the substantial threat to public health or welfare of a discharge of oil or a hazardous substance.[38] This can be accomplished by removing the discharged oil or hazardous substances; preventing threats of discharges; directing or monitoring federal, state, and private actors to remove a discharge; or removing or, if necessary, destroying a discharging vessel.[39] The CWA also provides that if the President determines that there may be an imminent and substantial threat to the public health or welfare because of an actual or threatened discharge of a hazardous substance, the federal government may secure relief through the issuance of an administrative order or through the commencement of a judicial action by the Department of Justice.[40]

If the removal is performed by the United States, the owner or operator of the vessel or facility from which the oil or hazardous substance was discharged in violation of section 311(b)(3) is liable for the actual costs of removal incurred, with limitations outlined in the CWA.[41] These provisions cap the liability of a vessel owner at an amount calculated by reference to the size of the vessel, and the liability of an onshore facility owner at $50 million. These limits do not apply if the discharges resulted from "willful negligence" or "willful misconduct" by the owner. As discussed later, OPA has increased these limits and also provides

36. *See* 33 U.S.C. § 1321(b)(8).

37. *In re* Oil Spill by the Oil Rig "Deepwater Horizon" in the Gulf of Mexico, on April 20, 2010, 21 F. Supp. 3d 657, 734–38 ¶ ¶ 492–500 (E.D. La. 2014).

38. *See* CWA § 311(c)(1)(A), 33 U.S.C. § 1321(c)(1)(A).

39. *See* CWA § 311(c)(1)(B), 33 U.S.C. § 1321(c)(1)(B).

40. *See* CWA § 311(e)(1)(A), (B), 33 U.S.C. § 1321(e)(1)(A), (B).

41. *See* CWA § 311(f), 33 U.S.C. § 1321(f).

a broader liability scheme, so it is the statute that the government generally utilizes for recovery of its costs of an oil spill cleanup. An owner/operator who was ordered to perform the removal and failed to properly carry out the order is subject to a civil penalty in an amount up to $48,762 per day of violation (as of 2021) or an amount up to three times the costs incurred as a result of the failure to comply with the order.[42]

Section 311 provides for defenses against liability if the discharge was caused solely by an act of God, an act of war, U.S. government negligence, the act or omission of a third party, or a combination of any of these. If the discharge is caused by a third party, such as by a vessel not carrying oil negligently crashing into another carrying oil, that third party can be liable for the costs of removal.[43]

The removal authority granted to the federal government by section 311 is generally used for oil spills. For hazardous substance spills into waters, EPA typically utilizes the broader cleanup authority of the Comprehensive Environmental Response, Compensation, and Liability Act (CERCLA).[44] CERCLA authority, however, does not extend to oil releases.[45]

9.5 The Prevention of Prohibited Oil Discharges

In addition to prohibiting oil discharges and requiring notice if a discharge occurs, the CWA also requires measures from certain owners and operators to prevent oil discharges. Owners and operators of onshore and offshore facilities that have discharged or could reasonably be expected to discharge oil in harmful quantities, or that have oil storage capacities over specified minimums, are required to develop a Spill Prevention, Control, and

42. *See* CWA § 311(b)(7)(B), 33 U.S.C. § 1321(b)(7)(B), with adjustments for inflation. *See* 40 C.F.R. § 19.4 (EPA inflation-adjusted penalties).

43. *See* CWA § 311(g), 33 U.S.C. § 1321(g).

44. *See* 42 U.S.C. §§ 9601–9675.

45. *See id.* § 9601(14) (excluding petroleum from CERCLA's definition of "hazardous substance").

Countermeasures (SPCC) plan.[46] The requirements of these plans, and the necessary approvals, are discussed in detail at 40 C.F.R. part 112.

The SPCC plan must be "prepared in accordance with good engineering practices" and "have the full approval of management at a level of authority to commit the necessary resources."[47] The plan must provide for containment structures to prevent discharged oil from reaching a navigable water.[48] If containment is not practicable, the SPCC plan must contain an oil spill contingency plan and a commitment of resources to address any spill.[49] The plan must provide for training of personnel on oil spill prevention.[50] The SPCC regulations contain additional requirements if the facility has bulk storage tanks, pipes and other oil transfer operations, truck- and tank-car-loading racks, or oil production operations.[51] The owner or operator of any non-transportation-related onshore facility that could reasonably be expected to cause substantial harm to the environment by discharging oil also must prepare and submit a facility response plan to the regional administrator of the appropriate EPA regional office.[52] In addition, that owner/operator also must develop and implement a facility response training program and a drill/exercise program.[53]

9.6 A Summary of OPA

In addition to amending section 311, OPA established a comprehensive scheme for addressing oil spills. Among other features, OPA (1) establishes an Oil Spill Liability Trust Fund;[54] (2) provides for use of the fund to pay for federal or state removal costs and federal, state, or tribal costs of assessing and restoring damages

46. Facilities at which the above-ground capacity is 1,320 gallons or less of oil and the buried storage capacity is 42,000 gallons or less of oil are not subject to the SPCC Plan requirements. *See* 40 C.F.R. § 112.1(d)(2).
47. *Id.* § 112.7.
48. *Id.* § 112.7(c).
49. *Id.* § 112.7(d).
50. *See id.* § 112.7(f).
51. *See id.* §§ 112.7(h), 112.8–112.11.
52. The guidelines for this facility response plan are found at 40 C.F.R. § 112.20.
53. *See id.* § 112.21.
54. *See* 26 U.S.C. § 9509.

to natural resources;[55] and (3) imposes liability, subject to limited defenses,[56] on responsible parties for removal costs and various types of damages, including damages to natural resources and to real or personal property.[57] Like section 311, OPA establishes caps on liability, although these caps are higher than in section 311 (for onshore facilities, the limit is $350 million, as opposed to $50 million in section 311). The caps do not apply if there was gross negligence, willful misconduct, or a violation of applicable federal safety regulations.[58]

OPA establishes liability for the responsible party of vessels or facilities from which oil is discharged, or that pose a substantial threat of discharge of oil, into or upon the navigable waters or adjacent shoreline or into the U.S. Exclusive Economic Zone.[59] The question of what "from which oil is discharged" means, and therefore which entity or entities are liable for civil penalties, was litigated in the *Deepwater Horizon* case.[60] In the 2010 *Deepwater Horizon* oil spill, the oil traveled from the oil reservoir (BP and Anadarko were the owners/operators), up the well casing, and was released into the ocean through the riser and blowout preventer (part of the Transocean's *Deepwater Horizon* vessel). The district court held that "from" meant where the uncontrolled movement of oil began (which it found to be the well owned/operated by BP and Anadarko), and did not necessarily mean the point where the oil entered the marine environment, as the riser and blowout preventer (part of Transocean's vessel) were merely the conduit through which the oil moved.[61] The Fifth Circuit affirmed.[62]

Under OPA's expanded liability provisions, responsible parties are liable both for the costs of responding to the release of oil and for damages arising from the discharge. The categories of damages include:

---

55. *See* OPA § 1012, 33 U.S.C. § 2712.
56. *See* OPA § 1003, 33 U.S.C. § 2703.
57. *See* OPA § 1002, 33 U.S.C. § 2702.
58. *See* OPA § 1004, 33 U.S.C. § 2704.
59. *See* OPA § 1002(a), 33 U.S.C. §2702(a).
60. *In re* Oil Spill by the Oil Rig "Deepwater Horizon" in the Gulf of Mexico, on April 20, 2010, 844 F. Supp. 2d 746, 757–58 (E.D. La. 2012).
61. *Id.*
62. *In re* Deepwater Horizon, 753 F.3d. 570 (5th Cir.), *reaff'd on reconsideration*, 772 F.3d 350 (5th Cir. 2014), *cert. denied*, BP Exploration & Prod., Inc. v. U.S., 135 S. Ct. 2893 (2015).

1. Injury to, destruction of, loss of, or loss of use of natural resources, which are recoverable by a United States trustee, a state trustee, an Indian tribe trustee, or a foreign trustee;
2. Loss of tax and other revenues by the United States, a state, or a political subdivision;
3. Net costs of providing increased or additional public services during or after removal activities, which are recoverable by a state or political subdivision of a state;
4. Injury to, or economic losses resulting from destruction of, real or personal property, which are recoverable by a person who owns or leases that property;
5. Loss of subsistence use of natural resources, recoverable by any claimant who uses the natural resources regardless of ownership or management of the resources; and
6. Loss of profits or earning capacity due to injury, loss, or destruction of real or personal property or natural resources.[63]

In short, OPA established a more comprehensive scheme for responding to oil spills, establishing a process for notifying the governmental entities responsible for releases of oil, creating a process for responding to the spill, and beefing up the damages and penalties for which a responsible party is liable.

63. OPA § 1002(b)(2), 33 U.S.C. § 2702(b)(2). The Supreme Court in *Robins Dry Dock & Repair Co. v. Flint*, 275 U.S. 303 (1927), precluded recovery for economic damage in admiralty where there was not a proprietary (ownership or leasehold) interest in the physically damaged property. However, based on OPA's text, the district court ruled in the *Deepwater Horizon* litigation that Congress intended OPA to allow recovery for economic losses resulting from or due to an oil spill, without regard to whether the claimant had physical damage to a proprietary interest. *In re* Oil Spill by the Oil Rig "Deepwater Horizon" in the Gulf of Mexico, on April 20, 2010 [As to Motions to Dismiss the B1 Master Complaint], 808 F. Supp. 2d 943, 959–60 (E.D. La. 2011), *aff'd on other grounds, In re* Deepwater Horizon, 745 F.3d 157 (5th Cir.), *cert. denied sub nom.*, Louisiana *ex rel.* Ballay v. BP Exploration & Prod., 135 S. Ct. 401 (2014).

10 Wet-Weather Discharges from Point Sources

In addition to the discharge of pollutants from industrial or publicly owned treatment works (POTW) point sources discussed in previous chapters, the Clean Water Act (CWA) regulates discharges from point sources that are caused by precipitation events, such as rainfall and snowmelt.[1] These "wet-weather discharges" include stormwater runoff, combined sewer overflows, and sanitary sewer overflows. The regulations, guidance, and policies addressing each of these types of discharges are discussed in this chapter.

10.1 Regulation of Stormwater

Stormwater is defined by the CWA's implementing regulations as stormwater runoff, snowmelt runoff, and surface runoff and drainage.[2] It includes runoff from unimproved land and impervious areas such as paved streets, parking lots, and rooftops. Stormwater is a leading cause of impairment to water bodies that do not currently meet water quality standards; left uncontrolled, these discharges can result in the destruction of fish, wildlife, and aquatic habitats, and can threaten public health by contaminating food, drinking water, and recreational waterways.[3] As discussed in

1. Precipitation also causes discharges of pollutants from nonpoint sources. These discharges are discussed in Chapter 11.
2. 40 C.F.R. § 122.26(b)(13).
3. *See generally* EPA, EPA-821-99-012, Preliminary Data Summary of Urban Storm Water Best Management Practices (Aug. 1999) (Section 4.0: Environmental

Chapter 2, the 1972 amendments to the Clean Water Act did not contemplate regulation of stormwater as it entered into "waters of the United States," presumably because it did not come from a traditional point source.[4] Eventually, however, it became apparent that much of the stormwater was itself from point sources and, thus, required regulation. The 1987 Water Quality Act provided for a two-phased approach to regulating stormwater. Phase I addressed those specific categories needing immediate attention; it required a National Pollutant Discharge Elimination System (NPDES) permit and implementation of stormwater prevention or management programs by October 1, 1994. Phase II addressed all other stormwater discharge point sources. The pertinent provisions of the Water Quality Act are set forth in section 402(p) of the CWA,[5] and the associated regulations are found at 40 C.F.R. § 122.26.[6]

10.1.1 The Phase I Program

The Phase I program identified specific sources of stormwater discharge thought to have the greatest potential to negatively affect water quality and required these sources to obtain NPDES permits.[7] Those sources were (1) stormwater discharge associated with certain industrial activity; (2) stormwater discharge from

Assessment), https://www.epa.gov/sites/default/files/2015-11/documents/urban-stormwater-bmps_preliminary-study_1999.pdf.

4. EPA initially viewed stormwater as a nonpoint source and thus exempted stormwater discharges from NPDES permitting requirements. *See* 40 C.F.R. §125.4 (1975). The D.C. Circuit held the exemption unlawful. Nat. Res. Def. Council v. Costle, 568 F.2d 1369, 1379 (D.C. Cir. 1977). Congress later enacted the Water Quality Act of 1987, which required NPDES permitting of stormwater discharges from industrial facilities, municipalities, and other sources. The Water Quality Act established specific timelines for the promulgation of new stormwater rules and to issue permits to dischargers. Environmental groups brought a number of challenges to EPA's rulemakings, prevailing in part. The challenges resulted in decisions that required EPA to finalize and beef up the rules. *See, e.g.*, NRDC v. EPA, 966 F.2d 1292 (June 4, 1992) (NRDC challenged EPA's extension of certain statutory deadlines; the court held unlawful EPA's failure to meet the statutory deadlines).

5. *See* CWA § 402(p), 33 U.S.C. § 1342(p).

6. For an overview of the stormwater program, see *NPDES Stormwater Program*, EPA, https://www.epa.gov/npdes/npdes-stormwater-program (last updated Aug. 6, 2020).

7. 55 Fed. Reg. 47,990 (Nov. 16, 1990).

medium[8] and large[9] municipal separate storm sewer systems (MS4s); and (3) a discharge deemed by the U.S. Environmental Protection Agency (EPA) administrator or a state to "contribute[] to a violation of a water quality standard or [to be] a significant contributor of pollutants to waters of the United States."[10]

10.1.1.1 Stormwater Associated with Industrial Activity

The regulations define "stormwater discharge associated with industrial activity" as the discharge from any conveyance used for collecting and conveying stormwater and directly related to manufacturing, processing, or raw materials storage areas at an industrial plant.[11] Although this provision is broad on its face, the regulations provide that any discharge otherwise excluded from the NPDES program cannot be recaptured by this provision.[12]

Specifically excluded from the phrase "stormwater discharge associated with industrial activities" is discharge originating in areas located at a facility that are separate from the facility's industrial activities, such as office buildings and accompanying parking lots, as long as the drainage from the excluded areas is not mixed with stormwater drained from included areas.[13]

EPA has identified 11 categories of facilities that are considered to be engaged in "industrial activity" for purposes of stormwater regulation.[14] These include (1) facilities subject to stormwater effluent limitation guidelines, new source performance standards, or toxic pollutant effluent standards; (2) facilities in various standard industrial classifications;[15] (3) hazardous waste treatment, storage, or disposal facilities; (4) landfills and dumps; (5) certain recycling facilities;[16] (6) steam electric power–generating facilities;

8. A "medium" MS4 generally is one that serves a population of 100,000 or more but less than 250,000. *See* 40 C.F.R. § 122.26(b)(7).

9. A "large" MS4 generally is one that serves a population of 250,000 or more. *See* 40 C.F.R. § 122.26(b)(4).

10. Also included among these sources were stormwater discharges for which a permit was issued before February 4, 1987. *See* CWA § 402(p)(1), (2), 33 U.S.C. § 1342(p)(1), (2); 40 C.F.R. § 122.26(a)(1)(i).

11. *See* 40 C.F.R. § 122.26(b)(14).

12. *Id.*

13. *Id.*

14. These categories are found at 40 C.F.R. § 122.26(b)(14)(i)–(xi).

15. *See* 40 C.F.R. § 122.26(b)(14)(ii)–(iii) for relevant SIC codes.

16. *See* 40 C.F.R. § 122.26(b)(14)(vi).

and (7) certain transportation facilities.[17] Categorical examples of stormwater discharges from industrial activity include stormwater discharges from industrial plant yards, manufacturing buildings, storage areas (including tank farms), rail lines used to transport materials, and areas where industrial activity has taken place in the past and at which significant materials[18] remain and are exposed to stormwater.[19]

Industrial activity stormwater dischargers of stormwater to a MS4 must obtain their own NPDES permit, separate and apart from a permit issued to the municipality for its MS4 discharges. Permits for industrial discharges must meet all applicable provisions of both section 402 and section 301 of the CWA,[20] including the requirement that the discharge "achiev[e] . . . any more stringent limitation, including those necessary to meet water quality standards, treatment standards, or schedules of compliance, established pursuant to any State law or regulations (under authority preserved by [33 U.S.C. § 1370])."[21] In other words, industrial discharges must comply strictly with state water quality standards. (Compare this with the standards for municipal stormwater discharges, discussed next.)

10.1.1.2 Stormwater Discharge from Large and Medium Municipal Separate Storm Sewer Systems

Municipalities must obtain a permit for all discharges from large and medium MS4s.[22] The word "separate" in "municipal separate storm sewer systems" is intended to distinguish such systems from those older systems that have "combined" sewer systems, meaning they collect stormwater and wastewater together. An MS4

---

17. *See id.* § 122.26(b)(14)(viii).

18. The definition of "significant materials" includes, but is not limited to: raw materials; fuels; materials such as solvents, detergents, and plastic pellets; finished materials such as metallic products; raw materials used in food processing or production; hazardous substances designated under section 101(14) of the Comprehensive Environmental Response, Compensation, and Liability Act; any chemical the facility is required to report pursuant to section 313 of title III of the Superfund Amendments and Reauthorization Act of 1986 (the Toxics Release Inventory); fertilizers; pesticides; and waste products such as ashes, slag, and sludge that have the potential to be released with stormwater discharges. 40 C.F.R. § 122.26(b)(12).

19. *See id.* § 122.26(b)(14).

20. *See* CWA § 402(p)(3)(A), 33 U.S.C. § 1342(p)(3)(A).

21. CWA § 301(b)(1)(C), § 1311(b)(1)(C).

22. 40 C.F.R. § 122.26(a)(3)(i). 40 C.F.R. § 122.26(a)(3)(iii) and (iv) outline the municipal stormwater discharge permit application process.

is defined as a conveyance or system of conveyances (including roads with drainage systems, municipal streets, catch basins, curbs, gutters, ditches, manmade channels, or storm drains) that are (1) owned or operated by a state, city, town, borough, county, parish, district, association, or other public body having jurisdiction over disposal of sewage, industrial wastes, storm water, or other wastes, including special districts under state law such as a sewer district, flood control district or drainage district, or similar entity, or an Indian tribe or an authorized Indian tribal organization, or a designated and approved management agency under section 208 of the CWA[23] that discharges to waters of the United States; (2) designed or used for collecting or conveying storm water; (3) which is not a combined sewer;[24] and (4) which is not part of a POTW.[25]

EPA may designate discharges from municipal separate storm sewers on a system-wide or jurisdictional basis, and may consider location, size, quantity, and any other relevant factor in making this decision.[26] Expressly excluded from this permitting requirement is agricultural stormwater runoff, which is exempted from the definition of point source in 40 C.F.R. § 122.2,[27] and certain discharges of stormwater runoff from mining operations, as well as discharges from all field activities or operations associated with oil and gas exploration, production, processing, or treatment operations or transmission facilities.[28]

A "large" MS4 is one located in an incorporated place with a population of 250,000 or greater, or within a specific county enumerated in appendix H of the regulations.[29] A "medium" MS4 is one located in an incorporated place with a population of at least 100,000 but fewer than 250,000, or within a county enumerated in appendix I.[30] In addition, EPA may designate a system that does

23. Section 208 set forth the CWA's initial framework for addressing nonpoint source pollution and is discussed in Chapter 11. See 33 U.S.C. § 1288; EPA, Nonpoint Source Control Program (not dated), https://www3.epa.gov/npdes/pubs/nonpoint.txt (last visited July 19, 2021).

24. A combined sewer system is a conveyance that discharges stormwater runoff combined with municipal sewage. These are point sources that must obtain NPDES permits in accordance with 40 C.F.R. § 122.21. *See id.* § 122.26(a)(7).

25. *Id.* § 122.26(b)(8).

26. *Id.* § 122.26(a)(1)(A)–(D).

27. *See id.* § 122.26(a)(1)(v).

28. *See id.* § 122.26(a)(2).

29. *See id.* § 122.26(b)(4).

30. *See id.* § 122.26(b)(7).

not otherwise fall within these descriptions as a large or medium MS4 based on the interrelationship between the discharges of the designated storm sewer and the discharges from the MS4.[31] EPA also may determine that storm sewers located within the boundaries of a region defined by a stormwater management regional authority are considered to be a large or medium separate storm sewer system based on jurisdictional, watershed, or other appropriate criteria.[32]

EPA may issue either one system-wide permit covering all MS4 discharges within the large or medium system, or distinct permits for categories of discharges within the system.[33] These categories can be all discharges by the same municipality, discharges located within the same jurisdiction, discharges to the same watershed, or discharges that are similar in nature.[34]

The standards for municipal stormwater discharges differ from industrial activity stormwater discharges in that municipal discharges are not statutorily required to comply with all the provisions of section 301. Instead, Congress required permits for municipal storm sewer discharges "to reduce the discharge of pollutants to the maximum extent practicable, including management practices, control techniques and system, design and engineering methods, and such other provisions as the Administrator . . . determines appropriate for the control of such pollutants."[35]

---

31. *See id.* § 122.26(b)(4), (7). Factors that the administrator may consider in making the determination for large and medium systems are found, respectively, at 40 C.F.R. § 122.26(b)(4)(iii)(A)–(E) and 40 C.F.R. § 122.26(b)(7)(iii)(A)–(E).

32. *Id.* § 122.26(b)(4), (b)(7).

33. *Id.* § 122.26(a).

34. *Id.* § 122.26(a)(3)(ii).

35. CWA § 402(p)(3)(B)(iii), 33 U.S.C. § 1342(p)(3)(B)(iii). The Ninth Circuit in *Defenders of Wildlife v. Browner*, 191 F.3d 1159, 1165 (9th Cir. 1999), held that Congress's choice to require industrial stormwater discharges to comply with 33 U.S.C. § 301, but not to include the same requirement for municipal discharges, must be given effect. The case involved a challenge to NPDES permits to five municipalities, for their separate storm sewers, asserting the permits were illegal because they did not contain numeric limitations to ensure compliance with state water-quality standards. The court found that, given that the statutory language related to municipal discharges did not require compliance with 33 U.S.C. § 30, EPA had the authority to require less than strict compliance with state water-quality standards.

10.1.1.3 Discharges That Contribute to a Violation of a Water Quality Standard or That Are Significant Contributors of Pollutants to Waters of the United States

The designation of a discharge as one that contributes to a violation of a water quality standard or that is a significant contributor of pollutants to waters of the United States may include a discharge from any conveyance or system of conveyances used for collecting and conveying stormwater runoff or a system of discharges from MS4s.[36] However, it will not include discharges from mining operations not contaminated by mining operation products and discharges from all field activities or operations associated with oil and gas exploration, production, processing, or treatment operations or transmission facilities, which are exempt under 40 C.F.R. § 122.26(a)(2), or agricultural stormwater runoff, which is exempt from the definition of point source.[37]

10.1.2 The Phase II Program

The Phase II Final Rule[38] requires a permit for any discharge composed entirely of stormwater that did not require a permit under Phase I if the discharge is (1) from a small MS4 required to be regulated pursuant to 40 C.F.R. § 122.32;[39] or (2) a stormwater discharge associated with small construction activity.[40]

---

36. 33 U.S.C. § 1342(p).

37. *See* 40 C.F.R. § 122.26(a)(1)(v).

38. 64 Fed. Reg. 68,722 (Dec. 8, 1999).

39. *See* 40 C.F.R. § 122.26(a)(9)(i)(A), (e)(9)(i). A regulated small MS4 is any small MS4 located in an urbanized area (UA) as defined by the Bureau of the Census, or located outside of a UA and brought into the program by the NPDES permitting authority. *See* 40 C.F.R. § 122.32(a); EPA, EPA 833-F-00-01, Stormwater Phase II Final Rule: An Overview (revised Dec. 2005), https://www.epa.gov/sites/default/files/2015-11/documents/fact1-0.pdf.

40. *See* 40 C.F.R. § 122.26(a)(9)(i)(B), (e)(8). Stormwater discharge associated with small construction activity means the discharge of stormwater from construction activities, including clearing, grading, and excavating, that result in land disturbance of equal to or greater than one acre and less than five acres. It also includes the disturbance of less than one acre of total land area that is part of a larger common plan of development or sale if the larger common plan will ultimately disturb equal to or greater than one acre and less than five acres. It does not include routine maintenance that is performed to maintain the original line and grade, hydraulic capacity, or original purpose of the facility. The requirement for this subcategory can be waived if conditions found in 40 C.F.R. § 122.26(b)(15)(A)–(B) are met. Stormwater discharge associated with small construction activity also includes any other construction activity designated by EPA based on the potential for contribution to a violation of a water quality standard or for significant contribution of pollutants to waters of the United States. *See id.* § 122.26(b)(15).

In addition, the Phase II Final Rule requires an NPDES permit for a discharge:

- determined by the relevant NPDES permitting authority to require stormwater controls based on wasteload allocations that are part of total maximum daily loads (TMDLs) that address the pollutant of concern; or
- determined by the relevant NPDES permitting authority to contribute to a violation of a water quality standard or is a significant contributor of pollutants to waters of the United States[41] (This is commonly referred to EPA's "residual designation authority").[42]

Operators of such discharges must submit a permit application within 180 days of receiving notice.[43]

Small MS4 operators are required to develop a stormwater management system to reduce the discharge of pollutants "to the maximum extent practicable," and to meet water quality requirements, typically through best management practices.[44] The program must include six minimum control measures: (1) public education and outreach; (2) public participation; (3) illicit discharge detection and elimination; (4) construction site runoff control; (5) postconstruction runoff control; and (6) pollution prevention/ good housekeeping.[45] The requirements for small construction activity are established on a state-by-state basis.[46]

The Phase II Final Rule also revised the "no exposure" exclusion[47]—the NPDES stormwater regulations now exclude

---

41. 40 C.F.R. § 122.26(a)(9)(i)(C)–(D).
42. *Id.*
43. *Id.* § 122.26(a)(9)(iii).
44. *Id.* § 122.34(a); *see* EPA, 833-F-00-002, Stormwater Phase II Final Rule: Small MS4 Stormwater Program Overview (revised Dec. 2005), https://www.epa.gov/sites/default/files/2015-11/documents/fact2-0.pdf.
45. 40 C.F.R. § 122.34(b)(1)–(6).
46. *See* EPA, 833-F-00-013, Stormwater Phase II Final Rule: Small Construction Program Overview (revised Dec. 2005), https://www.epa.gov/sites/default/files/2015-11/documents/fact3-0.pdf.
47. The original no-exposure provision was found at 40 C.F.R. § 122.26(b)(14)(xi) and applied to certain facilities referred to as "light industry." *See* EPA, 833-F-00-015, Stormwater Phase II Final Rule: Conditional No Exposure Exclusion for Industrial Activity (revised Dec. 2005), https://www.epa.gov/sites/default/files/2015-11/documents/fact4-0-2.pdf. In 1992, the Ninth Circuit remanded to

stormwater discharges from all industrial facilities that have "no exposure" of industrial activities or materials to stormwater, except for discharges from construction activities disturbing five or more acres and discharges associated with small construction activity.[48] These facilities are required to complete, sign, and submit a no-exposure certification to the permitting authority once every five years. The Phase II Final Rule also added federal systems, such as military bases and correctional facilities, to the definition of small MS4s.[49]

EPA initiated a Phase III rulemaking to establish national performance or design requirements that could be achieved using green infrastructure, among other things, for newly developed and redeveloped sites. However, in 2014, EPA changed gears and stated that rather than revising the stormwater program, it would provide technical and financial incentives to encourage communities to improve their stormwater programs.[50]

10.2 Application Requirements

Application requirements for permits for stormwater discharges associated with industrial activity and small construction activity are found at 40 C.F.R. § 122.26(c). Application requirements for large and medium MS4 discharges are set forth at 40 C.F.R. § 122.26(d). Application deadlines are set forth at 40 C.F.R. § 122.26(e).

EPA for further rulemaking, a portion of the definition of "storm water discharge associated with industrial activity" that excluded the category of industrial activity identified as "light industry" when industrial materials and/or activities were not exposed to storm water. The court was concerned that an operator would determine for itself that there was "no exposure" and then simply not apply for a permit without any further action. NRDC v. EPA, 966 F.2d 1292, 1305 (9th Cir. 1992). As a result of the remand, EPA revised the "no exposure" provision so that the person responsible for a point source discharge from a "no exposure" industrial source must meet the conditions of the exclusion (described in preceding text), and complete, sign and submit the certification to the permitting authority.

48. 40 C.F.R. § 122.26(g).

49. *Id.* § 122.26(b)(16)(iii).

50. EPA, *NPDES Proposed National Rulemaking to Strengthen the Stormwater Program-Information Collection Request*, https://www.epa.gov/npdes/proposed-national-rulemaking-strengthen-stormwater-program-information-collection-request (last updated June 21, 2022).

10.3 Combined Sewer Overflows

Combined sewer systems are sewers that are designed to collect rainwater runoff, domestic sewage, and industrial wastewater in the same pipe. Historically, communities built these systems to collect both stormwater runoff and sanitary sewage in the same pipe. At a time when neither wastewater nor stormwater was being treated, such combined conveyances made sense. Today, however, they present major engineering challenges: while the system works to collect and transport wastewater to a treatment plant in dry weather, wet-weather conditions add volume that can exceed the capacity of the system and therefore must overflow through whatever means is available, typically through mechanisms that bypass the treatment plant and discharge directly into nearby streams, rivers, lakes, or estuaries. These combined sewer overflows (CSOs) consist of mixtures of domestic sewage, industrial and commercial wastewaters, and stormwater runoff.[51] CSOs often contain high levels of suspended solids, pathogenic microorganisms, toxic pollutants, floatables, nutrients, oxygen-demanding organic compounds, oil and grease, and other pollutants. CSOs are among the primary culprits for beach closings and shellfish restrictions.[52] While the obvious solution is for municipalities to construct separate sewer systems, many municipalities have cited the cost of doing so as being prohibitively expensive.[53]

In 1989, EPA released a National Combined Sewer Overflow Control Strategy, which affirmed that CSOs are "point sources subject to NPDES permit requirements including both technology-based and water quality–based requirements of the CWA."[54] On April 19, 1994, EPA published the Combined Sewer Overflow (CSO) Control Policy,[55] which provides guidance on how communities with combined sewer systems can meet CWA goals in

51. *See generally* EPA, *Combined Sewer Overflows (CSOs)*, https://www.epa.gov/npdes/combined-sewer-overflows-csos (last updated Nov. 23, 2021).

52. *See generally* EPA, *Combined Sewer Overflow Frequent Questions*, https://www.epa.gov/npdes/combined-sewer-overflow-frequent-questions (last updated Aug. 24, 2020).

53. *See, e.g.*, *NPDES Stormwater Cost Survey*, California State Water Resources Control Board, Prepared by Office of Water Programs California State University, Sacramento (Jan. 2005), https://www.waterboards.ca.gov/sandiego/water_issues/programs/stormwater/docs/wqip/2013-0001/J_References/J038.pdf.

54. 54 Fed. Reg. 37,370, 37,371 (Sept. 8, 1989).

55. 59 Fed. Reg. 18,688 (Apr. 19, 1994).

a flexible and cost-effective manner. Congress incorporated the policy into the CWA at section 402(q),[56] which requires that all permits issued to a municipal combined storm and sanitary sewer conform to the policy.[57]

The policy is intended to provide clear levels of control to meet health and environmental objectives; to provide sufficient flexibility to municipalities, especially financially disadvantaged communities; to consider the site-specific nature of CSOs and determine the most cost-effective means of reducing pollutants and meeting CWA objectives and requirements; to allow a phased approach to implementation of CSO controls considering a community's financial capability; and to review and revise water quality standards and their implementation procedures when developing CSO control plans to reflect site-specific wet-weather impacts of CSOs.[58]

The policy established January 1, 1997, as the deadline for implementing the minimum technology-based controls, referred to as the "nine minimum controls." These are measures that can reduce the prevalence and impacts of CSOs and that are not expected to require significant engineering studies or major constructions. They are:

1. Proper operation and regular maintenance programs for the sewer system and the CSOs;
2. Maximum use of the collection system for storage;
3. Review and modification of pretreatment requirements to ensure CSO impacts are minimized;
4. Maximization of flow to the POTW for treatment;
5. Prohibition of CSOs during dry weather;
6. Control of solid and floatable materials in CSOs;
7. Pollution prevention;

56. CWA § 402(q), 33 U.S.C. § 1342(q).

57. Section 402(q) also required that EPA report to Congress on the success of the CSO program. EPA submitted the report in January 2002. EPA, EPA 833-R-01-003, Report to Congress, Implementation and Enforcement of the Combined Sewer Overflow Control Policy (Dec. 2001), https://www3.epa.gov/npdes/pubs/csortcexecsum.pdf. The report found "substantial progress and investments in CSO control" resulting in "public health and water quality benefits.

58. 59 Fed. Reg. at 18,689.

8. Public notification to ensure that the public receives adequate notification of CSO occurrences and CSO impacts;
9. Monitoring to effectively characterize CSO impacts and the efficacy of CSO controls.[59]

In addition to these minimum controls, communities with combined sewer systems are also expected to develop long-term CSO control plans that will ultimately provide for full compliance with the CWA, including attainment of water quality standards.[60]

10.4 Sanitary Sewer Overflows

In contrast to combined sewer systems, sanitary sewer systems are designed to collect and transport only sewage, and not stormwater. When these systems are overloaded—either from insufficient engineering, infiltration and inflow of wet-weather runoff somewhere in the system, pipe or equipment failures, and/or deterioration of the system—sanitary sewer overflows (SSOs) can occur. SSOs are discharges of raw sewage from sanitary sewer systems, and can release sewage into basements or out of manholes and into city streets, playgrounds, and streams. EPA estimates that there are anywhere from 23,000 to 75,000 SSOs per year.[61]

SSOs, as with any other unpermitted discharge, are prohibited under section 301 of the CWA. Because even exemplary municipal collection systems, however, may experience unauthorized discharges, NPDES permits may contain a framework to evaluate circumstances of SSOs that result in a discharge, and may excuse them either through enforcement discretion or through the establishment of an affirmative defense.[62]

59. *Id.* at 18,691.
60. *See id.* at 18,691–94.
61. EPA, *Sanitary Sewer Overflows (SSOs)*, https://www.epa.gov/npdes/sanitary-sewer-overflows-ssos (last updated July 10, 2021).
62. *See, e.g.*, 40 C.F.R. § 122.41(m) (describing conditions when permitting authority should not pursue enforcement action for bypasses of waste treatment system); *id.* § 122.41(n) (setting forth requirements for "upset" affirmative defense).

10.5 Integrated Planning

As discussed in Chapter 7, wet-weather issues such as combined sewer overflows and sanitary sewer overflows have long been a focus of EPA's enforcement agenda, and "keeping raw sewage and contaminated stormwater out of the nation's waters" was identified on EPA's lists of National Enforcement Initiatives for both the 2014–2016 cycle[63] and the 2017–2019 cycle.[64] EPA may use its enforcement authority in either the administrative and judicial contexts, and often enters consent decrees aimed at ensuring compliance with parties in violation of their NPDES permits.[65]

Consent decrees often require the participating municipality to undertake long-term programs and projects to come into compliance. In an effort to assist communities in prioritizing their water quality goals, EPA has embraced integrated planning as a means of identifying efficiencies from separate wastewater and stormwater programs in order to prioritize capital investments that achieve human health and water quality objectives.[66] Integrated planning can also lead to more sustainable and comprehensive solutions, such as green infrastructure, that improve water quality and provide other community benefits.[67] EPA released its Integrated Municipal Stormwater and Wastewater Planning Approach Framework in June 2012,[68] and in January 2019, the Water Infrastructure and Improvement Act (H.R. 7279) was

---

63. *See National Enforcement Initiatives for Fiscal Years 2014–2016: Keeping Raw Sewage and Contaminated Stormwater Out of Our Nation's Waters*, EPA, https://www.epa.gov/enforcement/national-enforcement-initiatives-fiscal-years-2014-2016-keeping-raw-sewage-and (last updated Oct. 28, 2020).

64. News Release, EPA, EPA Announces National Enforcement Initiatives for Coming Years (Feb. 18, 2016), https://archive.epa.gov/epa/newsreleases/epa-announces-national-enforcement-initiatives-coming-years.html.

65. See EPA, EPA National Enforcement Initiative: Keeping Raw Sewage and Contaminated Stormwater Out of Our Nation's Waters—Status of Civil Judicial Consent Decrees Addressing Combined Sewer Systems (May 1, 2017), https://www.epa.gov/sites/production/files/2017-05/documents/epa-nei-css-consent-decree-tracking-table-050117.pdf (identifying 45 civil consent decrees between EPA and municipalities across the country regarding combined sewer overflows).

66. *See* EPA, *Integrated Planning for Municipal Stormwater and Wastewater*, https://www.epa.gov/npdes/integrated-planning-municipal-stormwater-and-wastewater (last updated July 19, 2021).

67. *Id.*

68. *See* EPA, Integrated Municipal Stormwater and Wastewater Planning Approach Framework (June 5, 2012), https://www.epa.gov/sites/production/files/2015-10/documents/integrated_planning_framework.pdf.

enacted, which added section 402(s) to the CWA to define "integrated plan" as one developed in accordance with that framework.[69] Integrated planning does not change existing regulatory or permitting standards or alleviate CWA compliance obligations, but rather is a tool that "will take advantage of the flexibilities in existing EPA regulations, policies and guidance to allow municipalities to sequence implementation of their CWA obligations to protect water quality and public health."[70]

69. Pub. L. No. 115-436, § 3, 132 Stat. 5558, 5558; see also EPA, Implementation of Integrated Planning in Accordance with the 2019 Water Infrastructure Improvement Act (WIIA) (Dec. 3, 2019), https://www.epa.gov/sites/production/files/2020-01/documents/wiia_integrated_planning_implementation_memo_december_2019_508.pdf.

70. *Integrated Planning Frequent Questions*, EPA, https://www.epa.gov/npdes/integrated-planning-frequent-questions (last updated July 15, 2021).

11 Reducing Nonpoint Source Pollution

11.1 Introduction

While the core of the Clean Water Act (CWA) is the prohibition of discharges from point sources unless otherwise permitted (usually through the National Pollutant Discharge Elimination System (NPDES) process), so-called nonpoint source (NPS) pollution is a leading cause of water quality issues throughout the United States.[1] The CWA does not contain a direct prohibition of discharges from nonpoint sources. This is because, historically, regulation of nonpoint sources appeared too difficult to create and enforce. Nonetheless, NPS is uniformly believed to be one of "the largest remaining threat[s] to water quality and source[s] of water quality impairments in the nation," and therefore among the greatest obstacles to achievement of the goals of the Clean Water Act.[2]

NPS pollution is ubiquitous, ranging from urban stormwater to agricultural runoff and atmospheric deposition. Nutrient and sediment loading from agriculture and stormwater are significant contributors to "headlining" water quality problems such as hypoxia in the Gulf of Mexico[3] and decreased fish populations

1. *See* EPA, *Basic Information about Nonpoint Source (NPS) Pollution*, https://www.epa.gov/nps/basic-information-about-nonpoint-source-nps-pollution (last updated July 8, 2021); *see also* EPA, *Polluted Runoff: Nonpoint Source (NPS) Pollution*, https://www.epa.gov/nps (last updated July 20, 2021).

2. 68 Fed. Reg. 60,653, 60,656 (Oct. 23, 2003).

3. "Scientists have determined that the summer 2017 Gulf of Mexico's hypoxic zone, sometimes referred to as the 'dead zone,' was the largest measurement since mapping of the zone began in 1985. This zone, an area of low-oxygen water (less than 2 ppm) that cannot sustain fish and marine life, covered . . . an area roughly

in the Chesapeake Bay.[4] These issues further caught the nation's attention in 2017, when hot and dry conditions coincided with elevated nutrient levels in surface waters to create harmful algal blooms in waters from California to New Hampshire to Florida.[5]

Thus, addressing NPS pollution has become a major focus in attempting to meet the goals of the CWA. Indeed, the U.S. Environmental Protection Agency (EPA) in May 2011 identified implementation of initiatives to address polluted runoff—one of "our nation's highest water quality challenges"—as a CWA implementation priority for fiscal years 2011 to 2013.[6] Most recently, EPA has prioritized "market-based programs" for managing NPS pollution.[7]

As discussed in Chapter 6, water quality–based standards and the use of total maximum daily loads (TMDLs) (which consider all loadings to a water body) have played an increasingly important role in controlling NPS pollution. And in EPA's 2015 "waters of the United States" rulemaking (discussed in Chapter 3), EPA emphasized—as a central component of its analysis of aquatic systems that have a "significant nexus" with navigable waters—that "[w]etlands and other similar waters in floodplain areas act as buffers that are among the most effective tools for mitigating nonpoint source pollution."[8]

---

equal to the size of New Jersey." EPA, *Special Focus: Nutrient Pollution and Algal Blooms—Summer 2017 Gulf of Mexico Hypoxic Zone Was Largest in Recorded History*, Nonpoint Source News-Notes, Mar. 2018, at 5, https://www.epa.gov/sites/production/files/2018-03/documents/102issue.pdf.

4. *See, e.g.*, EPA, EPA 841-R-10-002, Guidance for Federal Land Management in the Chesapeake Bay Watershed (May 12, 2010), https://www.epa.gov/sites/production/files/2015-10/documents/chesbay_guidance-all.pdf.

5. EPA, *Federal Resources Help Protect People and Wildlife from Harmful Algal Blooms*, Nonpoint Source News-Notes, Mar. 2018, at 9, https://www.epa.gov/sites/production/files/2018-03/documents/102issue.pdf.

6. CWA Action Plan Implementation Priorities: Changes to Improve Water Quality, Increase Compliance and Expand Transparency 12 (May 2011).

7. 84 Fed. Reg. 49,293, 49,294 (Sept. 19, 2019).

8. *See* 80 Fed. Reg. 37,054, 37,070 (June 29, 2015).

11.2 Nonpoint Source of Pollution

NPS is undefined in the statute and the implementing regulations, though the term is understood to encompass any source of water pollution or pollutant not associated with a discrete conveyance.[9] A primary cause of NPS pollution is runoff, described by EPA as "rainfall or snowmelt moving over and through the ground."[10] As runoff travels, it picks up and carries natural and human-made pollutants, depositing them into lakes, rivers, wetlands, coastal waters, and underground sources of drinking water. NPS pollution includes:

- Excess fertilizers, herbicides, and insecticides from agricultural lands and residential areas;
- Oil, grease, and toxic chemicals from urban runoff and energy production;
- Sediment from improperly managed construction sites, crop and forest lands, and eroding streambanks;
- Salt from irrigation practices and acid drainage from abandoned mines;
- Bacteria and nutrients from livestock, pet wastes, and faulty septic systems; and
- Atmospheric deposition and hydromodification.[11]

Nonpoint sources also include animal feeding operations that do not exceed the size thresholds (discussed in Chapter 3) defined in EPA's regulations that would render them concentrated animal feeding operations, and thus, point sources.[12]

---

9. *See* Nat. Res. Def. Council, Inc. v. EPA, 301 F. Supp. 3d 133, 137 n.1 (D.D.C. 2018).

10. *Basic Information about Nonpoint Source (NPS) Pollution*, *supra* note 1. Management of stormwater under the NPDES program is covered in Chapter 10.

11. *Id.* EPA has defined hydromodification as the "alteration of the hydrologic characteristics of coastal and non-coastal waters, which in turn could cause degradation of water resources." Examples of hydromodification in streams include dredging, straightening, and complete stream relocation. *See* EPA, EPA 841-B-07-002, National Management Measures to Control Nonpoint Source Pollution from Hydromodification 1-1 (July 2007), https://www.epa.gov/sites/default/files/2015-09/documents/hydromod_all_web.pdf; *see also* 40 C.F.R. § 401.11.

12. 40 C.F.R. § 122.23.

11.3 Nonpoint Source Pollution Addressed in the Clean Water Act

While the need for NPS pollution control was recognized in the 1972 amendments to the CWA, the ability to control and regulate such pollution has remained a challenge. The 1972 and 1987 amendments addressed NPS pollution as part of the required management plans under sections 208 and 319 of the CWA.

11.3.1 Section 208: Area-Wide Waste Treatment Management Plans

Section 208, originally enacted as part of the 1972 amendments, requires states to develop and implement area-wide waste treatment management plans. Section 208 functions as a planning provision rather than any sort of regulatory program. Each state, using the regulation guidelines issued by EPA, is required to identify each area within the state having substantial water quality control problems.[13] The governor then designates a single representative agency (which may be an existing or newly created local, regional, or state agency or political subdivision) to develop effective area-wide waste treatment management plans for each such area.[14] The designated representative organization generates and continually updates an area-wide waste treatment management planning process. This process must contain, among other things, the identification of NPS pollution and the proposed controls, including best management practices (BMPs),[15] to attain or maintain an approved water use.[16] The following NPS must specifically be addressed in the area-wide waste treatment management plan:

- Farming- and forestry-related NPS pollution, including return flows from irrigated agriculture, and their cumulative

---

13. *See* CWA § 208(a)(2), 33 U.S.C. § 1288(a)(2); *see* 40 C.F.R. § 130.6.
14. *Id.*
15. BMPs are measures, or practices, selected by an agency to meet its nonpoint source control needs. They include, but are not limited to, structural and nonstructural controls and operation and maintenance procedures. BMPs can be applied before, during, and after pollution-producing activities to reduce or eliminate the introduction of pollutants into receiving waters. 40 C.F.R. § 130.2(m).
16. *See id.* § 130.6(c)(4).

effects, runoff from manure disposal areas, and from land used for livestock and crop production;

- Mining-related sources of pollution, including new, current, and abandoned surface and underground mine runoff;
- Construction activity-related sources of pollution;
- Saltwater intrusion into rivers, lakes, and estuaries resulting from reduction of freshwater flow from any cause, including irrigation, obstruction, groundwater extraction, and diversion;
- Disposition of residual waste generated in the area;
- Disposal of pollutants on land or in subsurface excavations within such area to protect groundwater and surface water quality; and
- Urban stormwater.[17]

These plans are certified by the governor, then approved by the EPA administrator.[18]

11.3.2 Section 319: Nonpoint Source Management Programs

The 1987 amendments included the establishment of the Nonpoint Source Management Program under section 319, which provides states, territories, and tribes with grants to implement NPS pollution controls described in EPA-approved NPS pollution management programs.[19] EPA has described its vision of this program as follows: "All States and territories implement dynamic and effective nonpoint source programs designed to achieve and maintain beneficial uses of water."[20] From 1999 to 2020, EPA

---

17. CWA § 208(b)(1), (2)(F)–(K), 33 U.S.C. § 1288(b)(1), (2)(F)–(K); 40 C.F.R. § 130.6(c)(4).

18. *See* CWA § 208(b)(1)(B), (3), 33 U.S.C. § 1288(b)(1)(B), (3).

19. *See* 33 U.S.C. § 1329.

20. 68 Fed. Reg. 60,655 (Oct. 23, 2003) (guidance that applied from 2004 through 2013); *see also* EPA, Nonpoint Source Program and Grants Guidelines for States and Territories (Apr. 12, 2013) (guidance applicable to all section 319-fund grant activities beginning in fiscal year 2014), https://www.epa.gov/sites/default/files/2015-09/documents/319-guidelines-fy14.pdf; EPA, Applying for and Administering CWA Section 319 Grants: A Guide for State Nonpoint Source Agencies (Sept. 2019) [hereinafter Section 319 Grant Guidance], https://www.epa.gov/sites/production/files/2015-09/documents/319applying-guide-revised.pdf.

consistently issued between $150 million and $240 million in section 319 grants annually.[21]

To be eligible for a grant, a state, territory, or tribe must develop and obtain EPA approval of (1) an NPS pollution assessment report that identifies waters impacted or threatened by NPS pollution, as well as the categories of NPS pollution that are impacting the water; and (2) an NPS pollution management program that supports activities with the greatest potential to produce early, demonstrable water quality results, assists in the building of long-term institutional capacity to address NPS pollution problems, and encourages strong interagency coordination.[22] The requirements for participation in these programs are detailed in EPA grant guidelines for the program last issued in April 2013.[23] In those guidelines, EPA prioritizes the use of funds for developing and implementing plans that address NPS pollution on a watershed basis. All states and territories and more than 170 tribes have EPA-approved NPS management programs.[24] As a result of improvements in these programs, EPA had documented more than 1,300 water quality improvement "success stories" as of July 2021.[25]

11.3.3 Water Quality Trading

As discussed in Chapter 6, EPA has also supported market-based mechanisms to address water quality issues caused by NPS pollution. In particular, the Agency has interpreted the CWA to allow pollutant reductions from water quality trading and offsets to achieve compliance with CWA regulatory requirements including water quality–based effluent limitations.

In 2003, EPA issued a formal Water Quality Trading Policy, designed to encourage voluntary trading programs to facilitate implementation of TMDLs, reduce the costs of compliance with CWA regulations, incentivize voluntary reductions, and

21. EPA, *319 Grant Program for States and Territories*, https://www.epa.gov/nps/319-grant-program-states-and-territories (last updated Oct. 9, 2020).
22. *See* CWA § 209(a), (b), (h), 33 U.S.C. § 1329(a), (b), (h).
23. *See* Section 319 Grant Guidance, *supra* note 20.
24. *See* Section 319 Grant Guidance, *supra* note 20, at 7–8, 51; *see also* 68 Fed. Reg. at 60,655.
25. *See* EPA, *Success Stories about Restoring Water Bodies Impaired by Nonpoint Source Pollution*, https://www.epa.gov/nps/success-stories-about-restoring-water-bodies-impaired-nonpoint-source-pollution (last updated July 16, 2021).

promote watershed-based initiatives.[26] In an effort to modernize its approach to market-based programs, the EPA issued new guidance entitled, "Updating the Environmental Protection Agency's (EPA) Water Quality Trading Policy to Promote Market-Based Mechanisms for Improving Water Quality" (2019 Memorandum).[27] In that updated policy, EPA identified a series of principles that states, tribes, and stakeholders should consider in implementing water quality trading and other market-based programs on a watershed scale.[28]

In September 2019, EPA requested public comments on options for providing additional flexibilities for baselines for nonpoint sources in watersheds with EPA established or approved TMDLs. EPA proposed, among other things, that NPS should generate credits for pollutant reductions where a TMDL has been established for a particular waterbody.[29] EPA also sought comment on how water quality standard variances could be used to implement market-based programs.[30]

11.4 Coastal Zone Act Reauthorization Amendments of 1990

Another NPS management program was implemented by section 6217 of the Coastal Zone Act Reauthorization Amendments of 1990.[31] Section 6217 called for 29 coastal states and territories to establish new NPS programs to restore and protect coastal waters. The coastal states were to implement control programs for NPS in compliance with guidelines published by EPA in 1993.[32]

---

26. EPA, Water Quality Trading Policy (January 13, 2003), *in* Water Quality Trading Toolkit for Permit Writers, at B-2 (June 2009), https://www.epa.gov/sites/production/files/2016-04/documents/wqtradingtoolkit_app_b_trading_policy.pdf.

27. Updating the Environmental Protection Agency's (EPA) Water Quality Trading Policy to Promote Market-Based Mechanisms for Improving Water Quality, EPA Memorandum from David P. Ross, Assistant Administrator, to Regional Administrators 3–5 (Feb. 6, 2019), https://www.epa.gov/sites/production/files/2019-02/documents/trading-policy-memo-2019.pdf.

28. 84 Fed. Reg. 49,293, 49,295 (Sept. 19, 2019).

29. *Id.* at 49,296.

30. *Id.*

31. *See* 16 U.S.C. § 1455b.

32. Coastal Nonpoint Source Pollution State Program Guidance Document, 58 Fed. Reg. 5182 (Jan. 19, 1993).

In 1995, coastal states and territories submitted their coastal NPS programs to EPA and the National Oceanic and Atmospheric Administration for review and approval. Approved programs include several key elements. One is a description of how a state or territory plans to control NPS pollution. EPA requires that states and territories ensure that the management measures are actually implemented. Mechanisms for doing so can be permit programs, zoning, enforceable water quality standards, and general environmental laws and prohibitions. States and territories may also use voluntary approaches such as economic incentives if they are backed by appropriate regulations. In other words, the federal requirement for management plans can result in enforceable state rules that limit NPS pollution.

12 Enforcement

12.1 Introduction

As with other significant environmental statutes, Congress in crafting the Clean Water Act (CWA) recognized the importance of an enforcement scheme to ensure that the CWA's goals are met. Thus, section 309 of the CWA provides for a full range of enforcement options by the federal government, including criminal, civil, and administrative enforcement alternatives, as well as the ability to abate certain imminent and substantial endangerments. Moreover, section 505 of the CWA provides for broad citizen suit enforcement authority. Finally, although it does not provide directly for enforcement options to be implemented by states, the CWA does contemplate that, in the first instance, much of the relevant enforcement will be undertaken by states. The principal enforcement provisions are contained in sections 309, 504, and 505 of the CWA.[1]

12.2 Criminal Enforcement

Section 309(c) of the CWA contains four provisions—one misdemeanor and three felonies—under which the United States may criminally prosecute those who violate various provisions of the CWA.[2] The breadth of these provisions is one reason that

---

1. CWA §§ 309, 504, 505, 33 U.S.C. §§ 1319, 1364, 1365.
2. CWA § 309(c), 33 U.S.C. § 1319(c). The actual criminal sentence will be determined by the court based on the U.S. Sentencing Guidelines.

the Clean Water Act, together with the Resource Conservation and Recovery Act, is among the environmental laws most often enforced criminally.

The misdemeanor provision, section 309(c)(1),[3] allows for the prosecution of those who "negligently" violate various provisions of the CWA or the terms of permits issued under the CWA by the U.S. Environmental Protection Agency (EPA), the U.S. Army Corps of Engineers (in the case of section 404 permits), or an authorized state. Among the provisions for which a violation is potentially criminal is the general prohibition, contained in section 301, of discharges of pollutants to waters of the United States.[4] In other words, those who negligently discharge pollutants without a permit, negligently violate the terms of a permit, or negligently discharge to a sewage system and thereby cause Clean Water Act violations may be subject to criminal liability. Section 309(c)(1) additionally covers persons who negligently discharge into sewer systems in a manner that may cause personal injury or property damage, or cause the treatment works to violate its permit limitations. The CWA does not define the term "negligently"; however, the provision has been judicially interpreted to require proof only of ordinary negligence, not gross negligence, and has been upheld as constitutional notwithstanding this low threshold.[5] For negligent violations, the CWA provides for fines of up to $25,000 per day and up to one year imprisonment. For repeat violations, the maximum penalty is $50,000 per day, with imprisonment of up to two years.[6]

It bears emphasis that the misdemeanor provision, although based on negligence alone, can result in very large fines, because of the application of the Alternative Fines Act,[7] which provides that in any case where an offense results in "pecuniary gain" to the defendant or "pecuniary loss to a person other than the defendant" the court may impose a fine of not more than twice the gain or loss.[8] The federal government relied on this provision in

3. CWA § 309(c)(1), 33 U.S.C. §§ 1319(c)(1).

4. Section 301 and the scope of "waters of the United States" are discussed in Chapter 3.

5. United States v. Hanousek, 176 F.3d 1116 (9th Cir. 1999), *cert. denied*, 528 U.S. 1102 (2000).

6. CWA § 309(c)(1), 33 U.S.C. §§ 1319(c)(1). The actual criminal sentence will be determined by the court based on the U.S. Sentencing Guidelines.

7. 18 U.S.C. § 3571(d).

8. *Id.*

its prosecution of BP relating to the 2010 Deepwater Horizon oil spill. In that case, the government filed a multicount information in which the only Clean Water Act charge was a misdemeanor count for negligent discharges. The government noted in the Plea Agreement that the maximum fine was "twice the gross gain or loss," and the Plea Agreement allocated a fine of $1.15 billion to the Clean Water Act misdemeanor count.[9]

The first of the CWA's felony provisions—and the most often utilized criminal provision of the CWA—parallels the provision for negligent violations with the added requirement that the violation be "knowing," rather than negligent. The "knowing" requirement has been interpreted to require only the general intent that the person knowingly undertook the activity in question; the person need not know that the activity violated the law.[10] In the case of a knowing violation, section 309(c)(2)[11] provides a maximum fine of up to $50,000 per day ($100,000 per day for repeat violations) and imprisonment for up to three years (up to six years for repeat violations).

The second and most serious felony sanction is set forth in section 309(b)(3),[12] which addresses violative conduct that parallels the provisions for negligent and knowing violations, with the added requirement that the violator know at the time of violation that he or she has put another person in imminent danger of death or serious bodily injury. In such cases, the maximum fine is $250,000 ($1 million for organizations) with a maximum imprisonment of 15 years (which may be doubled for repeat violations).

Finally, section 309(c)(4) authorizes the imposition of criminal sanctions for persons who make "false and material statements, representations or certification" in documents filed or maintained under the CWA or who tamper with monitoring equipment maintained under the CWA.[13] Such persons are subject to fines of up to $10,000 or imprisonment for up to two years (again, these maximums may be doubled for repeat violations).

---

9. The Information is available at https://www.justice.gov/iso/opa/resources/73920121115143627533671.pdf. The Plea Agreement is available at https://www.justice.gov/iso/opa/resources/43320121115143613990027.pdf.

10. United States v. Weitzenhoff, 1 F.3d 1523 (9th Cir. 1993), *reh'g denied & opinion amended*, 35 F.3d 1275 (9th Cir. 1994).

11. CWA § 309(c)(2), 33 U.S.C. § 1319(c)(2).

12. CWA § 309(c)(3), 33 U.S.C. § 1319(c)(3).

13. CWA § 309(c)(4), 33 U.S.C. § 1319(c)(4).

The government may pursue criminal sanctions under the CWA against organizations and individuals, including responsible corporate officers.[14] The term "responsible corporate officer" is not defined in the CWA, and the extent to which violative conduct of a lower-level corporate employee will be attributed to and form the basis of prosecution of either corporate officials or the corporation itself is typically a case-by-case prosecutorial decision. There have been two significant decisions addressing the issue. In *United States v. Iverson,*[15] the government prosecuted the president and chairman of a company even though he did not himself commit the violative acts, arguing that he was present during the unlawful discharges and did not act to abate them. The Ninth Circuit rejected the defendant's argument that a corporate officer is not "responsible" when he or she does not exercise control over the illegal activity.[16] Similarly, in *United States v. Hong,* the Fourth Circuit upheld the conviction of a corporation's sole shareholder for negligent violations of the CWA's pretreatment requirements.[17]

12.3 Civil Enforcement

The CWA authorizes EPA to bring civil actions in federal district court for violations of the CWA, including unpermitted discharges, discharges in violation of technology-based or water quality–based effluent limitations, violations of new source performance standards, violations of reporting and record-keeping requirements, and discharges in violation of National Pollutant Discharge Elimination System (NPDES) and certain other permits. Specifically, section 309(b) allows for commencement of civil actions for "appropriate relief," including injunctions, for such violations.[18] Section 309(d) provides for penalties up to $25,000

---

14. *See* CWA § 309(c)(6), 33 U.S.C. § 1319(c)(6) (defining the class of persons subject to criminal liability to include "responsible corporate officers").
15. 162 F.3d 1015 (9th Cir. 1998).
16. 162 F.3d at 1025.
17. 242 F.3d 528 (4th Cir. 2001).
18. CWA § 309(b), 33 U.S.C. § 1319(b).

per day for each violation.[19] EPA also may seek such penalties for violations of any requirement in an approved pretreatment program.

12.3.1 Injunctive Relief

If a violation is continuing, the government generally will seek injunctive relief as authorized by section 309(b). In cases in which achieving compliance will require significant capital expenditure, such as upgrades to a sewage system, the relief sought may include imposition of a compliance schedule, requiring the defendant to install necessary improvements on a predetermined schedule. Where publicly owned treatment works (POTWs) have had long-standing compliance problems, the government in the past has sought and obtained more extensive injunctive relief aimed at facilitating compliance. These forms of injunctive relief have ranged from a ban on new sewer connections until compliance is achieved[20] to the appointment by the court of a special administrator to run the POTW.[21]

EPA has recognized that successful enforcement resolutions requiring significant capital expenditures need to take account of the potential impact of climate changes. In December 2016, at the end of the Obama administration, EPA issued its "Framework for Protecting Public and Private Investment in Clean Water Act Enforcement Remedies."[22] Among other things, EPA noted that for certain Clean Water Act enforcement actions involving industrial entities, it would seek to require preparation of a "vulnerability assessment" such as in cases where "there is proximity to water bodies and areas that may be impacted by flooding, storm surge, and sea level rise; capacity of the collection or treatment system to handle more frequent or more intense precipitation; and possible downstream impacts."[23] EPA might then require that the set-

19. CWA § 309(d), 33 U.S.C. § 1319(d). The $25,000 per day maximum has been adjusted to account for inflation and is presently $59,973 per day. 40 C.F.R. § 19.4.

20. *See* United States v. Metro. Dist. Comm'n, 930 F.2d 132, 134 (1st Cir. 1991).

21. *See* United States v. City of Detroit, 476 F. Supp. 512, 515 (E.D. Mich. 1979).

22. EPA, Framework for Protecting Public and Private Investment in Clean Water Act Enforcement Remedies (not dated), https://www.epa.gov/sites/default/files/2016-12/documents/frameworkforprotectingpublicandprivateinvestment.pdf (last visited July 20, 2021).

23. *Id.*

tling party "implement resilience and adaptation measures based on the results of these vulnerability assessments and the expected useful life of the infrastructure in question, as needed to ensure long-term compliance with the CWA."[24] The extent to which such vulnerability assessments and resilience measures are the subject of enforcement focus can change as EPA's political leadership changes from one administration to the next.

12.3.2 Civil Penalties

In addition to injunctive relief, the government typically seeks penalties for past violations. The statute of limitations for penalties is five years,[25] meaning the government can seek penalties for violations during the five-year prefiling period as well as for any post-filing violations. Given the statutory maximum of up to $59,973 per day,[26] and the fact that violations often continue for long periods of time, the maximum penalty can amount to millions of dollars. The CWA enumerates six factors for the court to consider in determining the precise amount of the civil penalty:

> [1] the seriousness of the violation or violations, [2] the economic benefit (if any) resulting from the violation, [3] any history of such violations, [4] any good-faith efforts to comply with the applicable requirements, [5] the economic impact of the penalty on the violator, and [6] such other matters as justice may require.[27]

Although courts consider each of these factors, the economic benefit factor is usually emphasized by the government, and it often plays a prominent role in judicial decisions. As one court noted, "[T]he goal of the economic benefit analysis is to prevent a violator from profiting from its wrongdoing."[28] In calculating the economic benefit, the government typically has focused on the delayed and avoided costs from delayed compliance. For example, if a facility has delayed installing necessary pollution controls, both the interest saved in not borrowing money to finance the equipment and the costs saved in not operating the equipment earlier would be components of the government's economic

24. *Id.*
25. 28 U.S.C. § 2462; *see* Section 12.8 *infra*.
26. 40 C.F.R. § 19.4.
27. CWA § 309(d), 33 U.S.C. § 1319(d).
28. United States v. Mun. Auth. of Union Twp., 150 F.3d 259, 263 (3d Cir. 1998); *see* Friends of the Earth, Inc. v. Laidlaw Env't. Servs. (TOC), Inc., 528 U.S. 167, 186 & n.2 (2000).

benefit calculation. The government also has pursued other methods of calculating economic benefit, including alleged "wrongful profits" obtained by the defendant during periods of operation in violation of the CWA. Accepting this approach, the Third Circuit found that the economic benefit could be measured by the profit realized from the increased production that the defendant pursued in spite of its resulting CWA violations.[29] The case involved a milk processor that had discharged wastewater in excess of applicable pretreatment standards. The district court calculated "wrongful profits" based on the company's decision to produce greater volumes of product, casing greater pollution, than it could produce in compliance. The court of appeals affirmed the district court's analysis and upheld the focus on "the economic benefits achieved by failing to reduce the volume of pollution created."[30] Courts generally have applied one of two methodologies in assessing penalties. In the "top-down" method, the statutory maximum penalty is determined and then reduced, as the court deems appropriate, based on mitigating factors—those of the six statutory factors that pointed to a lower penalty. Other courts use a "bottom-up" method, which begins with the economic benefit for noncompliance and then adjusts that number up or down based on the other statutory criteria. The Fourth Circuit applied the latter method in the *Smithfield Foods* case, which involved two swine slaughtering and processing plants that had discharged wastewater in excess of limits in an NPDES permit. The court found a $4.2 million economic benefit and tripled that amount to reach a total penalty of $12.6 million.[31]

More recently, the Fifth Circuit considered the appropriateness of an $81 million civil penalty that was assessed against CITGO Petroleum arising from an oil spill, where the district court had found that the economic benefit realized by CITGO was $91.7 million. The government argued that the district court had erred in assessing a penalty less than the economic benefit. The

29. *Mun. Auth. of Union Twp.*, 150 F.3d 259. EPA has a lengthy discussion of this in "Calculation of the Economic Benefit of Noncompliance in EPA's Civil Penalty Enforcement Cases," 70 Fed. Reg. 50,326, 50,330 (Aug. 26, 2005); *see also* 64 Fed. Reg. 32,948, 32,950 (June 18, 1999). In this document, EPA discusses a number of economic benefit approaches under the heading "Illegal Competitive Advantage."

30. 150 F.3d at 267.

31. United States v. Smithfield Foods, Inc., 191 F.3d 516 (4th Cir. 1999).

Fifth Circuit disagreed, because the bottom-up approach allows a district court to "adjust a penalty 'upward or downward' from the economic benefit calculation."[32] The district court, the Fifth Circuit observed, had apparently adjusted the penalty down "at least in part, on its consideration of CITGO's $65 million effort to clean up the spill."[33]

12.3.3 Settlement

Most civil enforcement cases are resolved through settlement. The settlements are embodied in judicial consent decrees and, if injunctive relief was sought, are lodged with the court for a 30-day public comment period.[34] Following the public comment period, the government may withdraw its consent based on the comments received, although that rarely happens. Otherwise, the United States will seek court approval and entry of the settlement.

EPA negotiates settlements in accordance with its Interim Clean Water Act Settlement Penalty Policy, issued on March 1, 1995 (Penalty Policy).[35] The Penalty Policy specifies computation of two components: (1) the economic benefit that EPA believes the defendant realized from the violation,[36] and (2) the "gravity" component, reflecting the seriousness of the violation and other factors. The gravity component is calculated for each month of violation, and incorporates factors and schedules to measure the "significance of violation" (including the percentage exceedance of permit limits), the "health and environmental harm" (including the impact on human health and aquatic environments), the "number of effluent limit violations," and the "significance of non-effluent limit violations."[37] The policy allows for a number of adjustment factors, including an upward adjustment if the violator is viewed as recalcitrant, and a downward adjustment for a quick

32. United States v. CITGO Petroleum Corp., 711 F. App'x 237, 239 (5th Cir. 2018).

33. *Id.*

34. 28 C.F.R. § 50.7. The notice of the settlement is published in the *Federal Register*, and also on the website of the Environment and Natural Resources Division of the Department of Justice. *See Proposed Consent Decrees*, U.S. Dep't of Just., https://www.justice.gov/enrd/consent-decrees (last visited Apr. 1, 2022).

35. Interim Clean Water Act Penalty Policy (Mar. 1, 1995), https://www.epa.gov/sites/default/files/documents/cwapol.pdf.

36. EPA uses a computer model called BEN for calculating economic benefit. *See* 70 Fed. Reg. 50,326 (Aug. 26, 2005); *see also* 64 Fed. Reg. 32,948 (June 18, 1999).

37. Interim Clean Water Act Settlement Penalty Policy, *supra* note 35, at 8–10.

settlement. The penalty may also be adjusted for certain litigation considerations, such as issues with the quality of the government's evidence.

One significant aspect of the Penalty Policy is its recognition that courts are unlikely to award very large penalties in cases that involve POTWs, usually run by municipalities, even though the POTWs may have long-standing violations. Often the cause of the violations is the difficult financial situation of the municipality. Thus, imposing substantial penalties on the municipality may undermine its future compliance. Because of this, the Penalty Policy features a separate provision involving municipalities, which allows for penalties that are significantly less than the economic benefit if the municipality made good-faith efforts to comply.[38]

An additional component that EPA may incorporate into settlements is a supplemental environmental project (SEP).[39] SEPs are defined by EPA "as environmentally beneficial projects which a defendant agrees to undertake, in settlement of an enforcement action, but which the defendant, or any other third party, is not otherwise legally required to perform." The use of SEPs is covered generally by EPA's SEP Policy (updated in 2015),[40] which allows a violator to perform certain types of environmentally beneficial projects—such as pollution reduction, pollution prevention, and environmental restoration—which it would not otherwise be required to do and, in essence, get a credit against its penalty. Defendants often prefer to perform SEPs because public perception of a defendant performing a SEP may be less stigmatizing than the payment of a penalty. EPA encourages the use of SEPs because of EPA's ability to, in essence, direct funds toward environmentally beneficial purposes, as opposed to a payment of penalties that is directed to the U.S. Treasury. In general, SEPs may be used to reduce the gravity component, but not the economic benefit component, of a penalty. In cases involving municipalities,

38. *Id.* at 17.

39. EPA's materials on SEPs are contained on its SEP webpage. *See Supplemental Environmental Projects (SEPs)*, EPA, https://www.epa.gov/enforcement/supplemental-environmental-projects-seps (last updated July 27, 2021).

40. EPA, Supplemental Environmental Projects Policy: 2015 Update (Mar. 10, 2015), https://www.epa.gov/sites/default/files/2015-04/documents/sepupdatedpolicy15.pdf; *see also* EPA Supplemental Environmental Project Policy (May 1, 1998).

however, SEPs are allowed even if the penalty being paid is less than the economic benefit.[41]

The use of SEPs decreased as a result of a number or policies issued by the Justice Department during the Trump administration, which first disfavored use of SEPs and then, in March 2020, precluded it.[42] But SEPs, which are often popular with both defendants and impacted communities, are expected to be back in favor during the Biden administration, and in February 2021, the Trump-era policies precluding SEPs were revoked, as were a number of other enforcement policies.[43]

12.4 Administrative Enforcement

The CWA also provides EPA with broad administrative enforcement authorities, which can be exercised in the first instance without going to court. Under section 309(a), EPA is authorized to require compliance by persons found to be in violation of the CWA or of any permits issued under the CWA. In addition, section 309(g) allows EPA to pursue penalties administratively for violations of the CWA or of permits.[44] The CWA divides into two classes the penalties that may be sought: (1) in Class I cases, EPA may seek penalties of up to $23,989 per violation, with a $59,973 cap; (2) in Class II cases, involving more serious violations, EPA may seek penalties of up to $23,989 per day, with a $282,293 cap.[45] In assessing penalties, EPA utilizes a list of criteria similar to those for judicial assessment of penalties.[46] Because the Clean Water Act imposes a relatively low maximum penalty that may be

41. Interim Clean Water Act Penalty Policy, *supra* note 35, at 22.

42. Env't & Nat. Res. Div., U.S. Dept. of Justice, Supplemental Environmental Projects ("SEPs") in Civil Settlements with Private Defendants (Mar. 12, 2020), https://www.justice.gov/enrd/file/1257901/download.

43. Env't & Nat. Res. Div., U.S. Dept. of Justice, Withdrawal of Memoranda and Policy Documents (Feb. 4, 2021), https://www.justice.gov/enrd/page/file/1364716/download.

44. CWA § 309(g), 33 U.S.C. § 1319(g).

45. CWA § 309(g)(2), 33 U.S.C. § 1319(g)(2); 40 C.F.R. § 19.4 (inflation-adjusted penalties).

46. EPA has promulgated regulations that govern administrative penalty proceedings, which can be found at 40 C.F.R. part 22.

sought administratively, the most substantial violations tend to be pursued judicially.[47]

The CWA provides for judicial review of agency penalty assessments, with Class I penalties reviewed in U.S. district court and Class II penalties reviewed in the U.S. court of appeals either for the District of Columbia Circuit or in the circuit where the alleged violator resides or transacts business.[48]

12.5 Emergency Authorities

The Clean Water Act, like other environmental laws, contains an "emergency powers" provision. Section 504 of the CWA allows EPA to bring suit in district court if it receives evidence "that a pollution source or combination of sources is presenting an imminent and substantial endangerment to the health of persons or to the welfare of persons where such endangerment is to the livelihood of such persons, such as inability to market shellfish."[49] If EPA brings a section 504 action, the court may issue appropriate orders, including one to abate the discharge of pollutants in question.[50] This provision has not been used with great frequency, in part because it is narrower in scope than similar provisions in other environmental statutes.[51] In particular, the provision does not allow EPA to issue administrative orders in these emergency cases.[52] Moreover, the statute requires EPA to put forth evidence that the pollution "is" presenting an endangerment, in contrast

47. In contrast to the Clean Water Act, the Resource Conservation and Recovery Act has no upper limit on penalties that can be sought administratively, 42 U.S.C. § 6928(a); and the Clean Air Act has a $200,000 cap for administratively imposed penalties, but that cap can be removed for a particular case by EPA and the Department of Justice, 42 U.S.C. § 7413(d).

48. CWA § 309(g)(8), 33 U.S.C. § 1319(g)(8).

49. CWA § 504, 33 U.S.C. § 1364.

50. *See* United States v. Vertac Chem. Corp., 489 F. Supp. 870 (E.D. Ark. 1980) (holding that escape of dioxin from a chemical manufacturing plant into waterways constituted "an imminent and substantial endangerment to the health of persons" and was subject to abatement under section 504).

51. *But see* United States v. Hooker Chems & Plastics Corp., 540 F. Supp. 1067 (W.D.N.Y. 1982) (approving settlement in case brought by EPA under section 504 and other environmental statutes against company responsible for landfill site where EPA found remedial measures to be insufficient); *Vertac Chem. Corp.*, 489 F. Supp. 870.

52. *See* CWA § 504, 33 U.S.C. § 1364.

to other statutes, which allow action when the pollution "may" present an endangerment. The endangerment must be to health or economic livelihood, as opposed to other statutes, which allow for action when there is a general threat to the environment.[53]

12.6 State Enforcement

Although the CWA does not directly provide for enforcement by states, three provisions contemplate such enforcement and address its ramifications. First, section 402(b) limits EPA's approval of state programs (which includes EPA's approval to the state to issue NPDES permits) to those cases where the state has adequate authority "[t]o abate violations of the permit or the permit program, including civil and criminal penalties and other ways and means of enforcement."[54] EPA's regulations contain further specification as to the type of enforcement authorities that a state must have in order to be able to issue NPDES permits.[55] Second, section 309(a) requires EPA to notify the state when it receives evidence that a person is in violation of a state-issued permit, and EPA can take action only if the state has not taken action during the following 30-day period.[56] Third, section 309(g)(6)(A) limits federal enforcement in certain cases where the state has taken an enforcement action.[57] In particular, it provides that violations "with respect to which a State has commenced and is diligently prosecuting an action under a State law comparable" to the administrative penalty provision of the CWA or for which the state has issued a final order and the violator

53. In comparison, the Resource Conservation and Recovery Act allows EPA to take action when conditions "may" present an imminent and substantial endangerment, the endangerment can be to "health or the environment," and EPA may issue administrative orders "as may be necessary to protect public health and the environment." 42 U.S.C. § 6973.

54. CWA § 402(b), 33 U.S.C. § 1342(b).

55. *See* 40 C.F.R. § 123.27. The state enforcement authorities do not need to mimic federal authorities precisely. For example, it is sufficient that a state have the authority to obtain penalties of $5,000 a day—well below EPA's authority of $25,000 a day.

56. CWA § 309(a), 33 U.S.C. § 1319(a).

57. CWA § 309(g)(6)(a), 33 U.S.C. § 1319(g)(6)(a).

has paid a penalty under a comparable state law may not be the subject of a federal civil penalty action under section 309.[58]

Thus, certain types of state enforcement actions can preclude later federal enforcement action. However, for these preclusion principles to apply, the state enforcement scheme must be "comparable" to that of the CWA. In the *Smithfield Foods* case, the court found that the state enforcement scheme was not comparable to section 309 and, therefore, federal action was not precluded.[59] In that case, Virginia did not have the authority to assess administrative penalties without the consent of the alleged violator and did not have comparable notice and public participation procedures.[60] An issue may also arise as to whether the state was "diligently" prosecuting its action.[61] While there are limitations on the preclusive effect of state enforcement on federal enforcement, as a practical matter EPA rarely "over files," meaning that when the state has taken enforcement action for any particular violation, it is very unusual for EPA to later take action with respect to the same violation.

12.7 Citizen Suits

Section 505 of the CWA allows citizens to commence suits in two very different situations: (1) against a regulated person for a violation of the substantive requirements of the CWA and (2) against EPA for failure to perform nondiscretionary acts or duties.[62]

12.7.1 Citizen Enforcement Suits

Section 505(a) of the CWA allows any citizen to commence a civil action on their own behalf against any person alleged to be

58. *Id.*

59. United States v. Smithfield Foods, Inc., 191 F.3d 516, 524 (4th Cir. 1999).

60. *Id.*

61. *See, e.g.*, United States v. Citgo Petroleum Corp., 723 F.3d 547 (5th Cir. 2013) (Louisiana Department of Environmental Quality's pending administrative action did not constitute diligent prosecution where at the time the U.S. filed its complaint, the administrative action "was pending but the attention being given to it was, at best, desultory" and Louisiana indicated that the State "would no longer pursue with diligence or otherwise the comparable relief being sought administratively.").

62. CWA § 505, 33 U.S.C. § 1365.

in violation of either an effluent standard or limitation or an EPA or state order with respect to such a standard or limitation. Before commencing a citizen suit, the citizens must provide 60 days' notice to EPA, the state, and the alleged violator.[63]

This citizen suit provision has been by far the most often invoked of those available under federal environmental laws, due in large part to the self-monitoring requirements of the CWA. That is, since NPDES permittees are required to monitor their discharge and to report to EPA or the issuing state on the monitoring, it is often a relatively simple matter for a citizen or citizen group to compare the reported effluent levels against limitations in the permit, and where the former exceeds the latter, commence a citizen suit.

Although the citizen suit provision in the CWA is broad, there are a number of important limitations. First, section 505(b) prevents the commencement of an action if EPA or the state has commenced and is diligently prosecuting a civil or criminal action for compliance with the standard or limitation at issue.[64] In such circumstances, however, the citizens are given the right to intervene in the pending enforcement action.[65] Second, while not specified in the statute, as a matter of constitutional law, the plaintiff must establish standing.[66] To do so, a plaintiff must show that the plaintiff has suffered an injury in fact that is concrete and actual or imminent,[67] that the injury can be traced to the defendant's conduct, and that the injury is likely to be redressed by a favorable decision.[68] In certain situations, environmental organizations or associations will have standing to represent the interests of their members.[69] Third, the Supreme Court has held that citizens may

---

63. CWA § 505(b), 33 U.S.C. § 1365(b).
64. CWA § 505(b)(2)(B), 33 U.S.C. § 1365(b)(2)(B).
65. CWA § 505(b)(2)(B), 33 U.S.C. § 1365(b)(2)(B).
66. Lujan v. Defs. of Wildlife, 504 U.S. 555 (1992).
67. The burden to establish standing is not an especially high one. The standard is not harm to the environment but harm to the plaintiff. For example, standing was upheld in one recent case involving water pollution from a pig farm because plaintiffs "alleged harm to their recreational, aesthetic, and commercial interests and they were within the area of contamination around the time of the discharge." Am. Canoe Ass'n v. Murphy Farms, Inc., 326 F.3d 505 (4th Cir. 2003).
68. *See* Friends of the Earth, Inc. v. Laidlaw Env't. Servs. (TOC), Inc., 528 U.S. 167, 180 (2000).
69. "An association has standing to bring suit on behalf of its members when its members would otherwise have standing to sue in their own right, the interests at stake are germane to the organization's purpose, and neither the claim asserted or the relief requested requires the participation of individual members in the

not bring suits alleging wholly past violations of the CWA. The Supreme Court has twice addressed this issue. In *Gwaltney of Smithfield, Ltd. v. Chesapeake Bay Foundation, Inc.*,[70] the Court found that because section 505 provided for claims against a person "who is alleged to be in violation" of the CWA, citizens may not sue solely for past violations. In that case, a citizen group alleged that the holder of an NPDES permit exceeded authorized effluent limitations in that permit. But due to the installation of new control equipment, the last reported violation occurred in May 1984, and the citizen enforcement lawsuit was not brought until June 1984. As the violations alleged were no longer continuing at the time the enforcement action was commenced, the Supreme Court held that the action should have been dismissed. More recently, in *Friends of the Earth, Inc. v. Laidlaw Environmental Services (TOC), Inc.*,[71] the Supreme Court held that if violations were continuing when a case was filed, the cessation of violations while the case was pending did not render the case moot.

12.7.2 Nondiscretionary Duty Suits

Section 505(b) authorizes a citizen suit against EPA in the event of a failure by the agency to perform a nondiscretionary duty.[72] This provision has been most often invoked when the CWA requires EPA to take a specific action by a specified date. It has been used frequently to compel the promulgation of total maximum daily loads (TMDLs).[73] If the decision being challenged is a discretionary one, however, a citizen suit may not be brought under section 505.[74] Litigation costs, including reasonable attorney and expert witness fees, may be awarded to any prevailing or substantially

---

lawsuit." *Id.* (citing Hunt v. Wash. State Apple Advert. Comm'n, 432 U.S. 333 (1977)).

70. 484 U.S. 49 (1987).

71. 528 U.S. 167 (2001).

72. This provision only allows actions against the administrator of EPA and has been interpreted not to allow similar suits against the Corps when it is exercising authority in connecting with section 404 permits. Nw. Env't. Def. Ctr. v. U.S. Army Corps of Eng'rs, 118 F. Supp. 2d 1115 (D. Or. 2000). *But see* Nat'l Wildlife Fed'n v. Hanson, 859 F.2d 313 (4th Cir. 1988) (citizens may enforce nondiscretionary duty of Corps when it is working in tandem with EPA).

73. *See, e.g.*, Columbia Riverkeeper v. Wheeler, 944 F.3d 1204 (9th Cir. 2019).

74. CWA § 505(a)(2), 33 U.S.C. § 1365(a)(2).

prevailing party, when the court determines that the award is appropriate.[75]

12.8 Defenses against Enforcement

The enforcement provisions of the CWA are very broad and preclude many possible defenses. In the civil context, the statute imposes strict liability independent of any intent or knowledge.[76] There are, however, several defenses available to alleged violators.

1. Fair notice. A defendant can assert that it did not receive fair notice of the legal requirement that it is alleged to have violated. In cases under other environmental laws, courts have ruled that a defendant cannot be penalized if it did not have fair notice of the applicable requirement, including where the regulatory language was ambiguous or confusing.[77]

2. Permit as a shield. An important defensive provision of the Clean Water Act is the "permit as a shield" provision of section 402(k), which provides that anyone in compliance with an NPDES permit is deemed in compliance with other major provisions of the CWA, including section 301.[78] Permittees thus can argue that if their discharge contained pollutants that were disclosed in the permit application, then the discharge of those pollutants is allowed, even if there is not a discharge limitation for that pollutant in the permit itself.[79]

3. "Upset" and "bypass." A defendant accused of violating its permit can sometimes allege, if the violations were caused by some unintended and unavoidable events, that the violation was caused by "upset" or was an allowed "bypass." Most permits contain a provision addressing "upset," which is defined as "an exceptional incident in which there is unintentional and

---

75. CWA § 505(d), 33 U.S.C. § 1365(d).

76. *See* Kelly v. EPA, 203 F.3d 519, 522 (7th Cir. 2000); United States v. Winchester Mun. Utils., 944 F.2d 301, 304 (6th Cir. 1991).

77. United States v. Hoechst Celanese Corp., 128 F.3d 216, 224 (4th Cir. 1997).

78. CWA § 402(k), 33 U.S.C. § 1342(k).

79. *See* E.I. du Pont de Nemours & Co. v. Train, 430 U.S. 112, 138 n.28 (1977); *see also* Atl. States Legal Found., Inc. v. Eastman Kodak Co., 12 F.3d 353, 357 (2d Cir. 1993).

temporary noncompliance with technology-based effluent limitations set forth in a permit because of factors beyond the reasonable control of the permittee."[80] The regulations greatly limit the use of the "upset" defense through a series of substantive and procedural requirements. To successfully invoke an upset defense, the permit holder must carefully document the cause of the upset and demonstrate that the facility was being properly operated at the time, that proper notice was given to the appropriate permitting authorities within 24 hours, and that required remedial measures were taken.[81] If permits issued pursuant to state law do not contain an upset provision, the defense cannot be invoked.[82] A "bypass" is an "intentional diversion of waste streams from any portion of a treatment facility."[83] It is primarily this intentional or preplanned nature that makes a diversion a "bypass," as opposed to an "upset," which is an unintentional exceedance. Under most circumstances, bypass is prohibited under the CWA, and EPA may take enforcement action against a permit holder for engaging in a bypass.[84] Bypass is allowed, however, when it is "unavoidable to prevent loss of life, personal injury, or severe property damage" and there are no "feasible alternatives" available.[85] Whenever possible, the permit holder must provide advance notice of any bypass to the appropriate authority.[86] In the case of unanticipated bypass, such as that resulting from a severe storm event, notification is required within 24 hours following the event.[87] This exception is intended to be very limited, and courts have consequently rejected attempts to expand its scope to include events such as routine maintenance.[88]

4. Statute of limitations. A civil enforcement action seeking only penalties is subject to the five-year federal statute of

80. 40 C.F.R. § 122.41(n)(1).

81. *See id.* § 122.41(n)(3).

82. *See* Sierra Club v. Union Oil Co. of Cal., 813 F.2d 1480, 1486 (9th Cir. 1987), *cert. granted, judgment vacated on other grounds, & case remanded,* 485 U.S. 931, *judgment reinstated,* 853 F.2d 667 (9th Cir. 1988).

83. *See* 40 C.F.R. § 122.41(m)(1)(i).

84. *See id.* § 122.41(m)(4)(i).

85. *See id.* § 122.41(m)(4)(i)(A), (B); *see, e.g.,* United States v. City of Toledo, 63 F. Supp. 2d 834 (N.D. Ohio 1999).

86. *See* 40 C.F.R. § 122.41(m)(3)(i).

87. *See id.* § 122.41(m)(3)(ii).

88. *See, e.g.,* United States v. Weitzenhoff, 1 F.3d 1523, 1532 (9th Cir. 1993), *reh'g denied & opinion amended,* 35 F.3d 1275 (9th Cir. 1994).

limitations for penalty actions.[89] This period begins to run from the time of violation (although if the violation is of a continuing nature, the statute of limitations will run separately for each day of violation). Although the government has argued that the time should run from its discovery of the violation, this "discovery rule" has been rejected by the courts.[90]

5. Laboratory error. The courts are divided as to whether a permit holder who has reported in its discharge monitoring reports that it has discharged in excess of allowable levels can assert, when enforcement commences, that there were not in fact exceedances, and that the discharge monitoring report was based on laboratory error. The United States has argued that a permittee should not be allowed to impeach its own reports, and this position was upheld in *Sierra Club v. Union Oil Co. of California*,[91] where a Ninth Circuit panel held that to allow permittees to defend enforcement by alleging laboratory error would "undermine the efficacy of the self-monitoring program." But the Third Circuit in *United States v. Allegheny Ludlum Corp.*[92] reached a contrary result, and found that laboratory error, if proven, would be a defense to permit violations. The court held that while the government could rely on the discharge monitoring reports to prove its case, the "trier of fact must still be convinced that the permit was in fact violated," and evidence showing that it was not violated because the reports overstated the level of discharge should be admitted.[93]

---

89. 28 U.S.C. § 2462; *see* United States v. Telluride Co., 146 F.3d 1241, 1245 (10th Cir. 1998); United States v. Banks, 115 F.3d 916, 918 (11th Cir. 1997).

90. *See* 3M Co. (Minn. Mining & Mfg.) v. Browner, 17 F.3d 1453, 1460 (D.C. Cir. 1994).

91. 813 F.2d 1480, 1491–92 (9th Cir. 1987), *cert. granted, judgment vacated on other grounds, & case remanded*, 485 U.S. 931, *judgment reinstated*, 853 F.2d 667 (9th Cir. 1988).

92. 366 F.3d 164 (3d Cir. 2004).

93. *Id.* at 174.

Table of Cases

R

S

T

U

Index